The Verse of Shao Xunmei

Heaven and May (1927) and Twenty-Five Poems (1936)

2. A portrait of Shao Xunmei painted by Xu Beihong in Paris in 1925.
邵洵美像,徐悲鴻作於 1925 年巴黎。

3. A picture of Shao Xunmei in Shanghai in 1924 provided by Shao Xiaohong, Shao's daughter.
月洞門前,手持書卷的邵洵美於 1924 年在上海;由邵洵美的女兒邵綃紅女士提供照片,特此感謝。

1. A cartoon of Shao Xunmei by his Mexican caricaturist, Miguel Covarrubias (1904-1957), in Shanghai in 1933.
1933 年，素有"漫畫王子"之稱的墨西哥漫畫家珂佛羅皮斯在上海為邵洵美所作的漫畫。

FIRST EDITION

Copyright © by Shao Xiaohong
English translation copyright © 2016 by Jicheng Sun & Hal Swindall
Published by arrangement with Shanghai Bookstore Publishing House

This publication is made possible with a grant from Shandong University of Technology of China.

All rights reserved. No part of this book may be reproduced, stored in a retrieval system, or transmitted in any form, or by any means, electronic, mechanical, photocopying, recording or otherwise, without prior permission from the publisher.

ISBN: 9781622460236
Cataloging-in-publication data available from the Library of Congress
www.loc.gov

Published by Homa & Sekey Books
3rd Floor, North Tower
Mack-Cali Center III
140 E. Ridgewood Ave.
Paramus, NJ 07652

Tel: 201-261-8810, 800-870-HOMA
Fax: 201-261-8890
Email: info@homabooks.com
Website: www.homabooks.com

Printed in U.S.A.
1 3 5 7 9 10 8 6 4 2

The Verse of Shao Xunmei
Heaven and May (1927) and Twenty-Five Poems (1936)

Translated by Jicheng Sun & Hal Swindall

洵美詩選

邵洵美 著

（中國）孫繼成 （美國）師文德 譯

Homa & Sekey Books
Paramus, New Jersey

4. Bookcover, *Heaven and May: The Collected Poems of Shao Xunmei* in 1927

邵洵美詩集《天堂與五月》封面，1927年1月出版。

5. Bookcover, *Twenty-Five Poems: The Collected Poems of Shao Xunmei* in 1936

邵洵美詩集,《詩二十五首》封面（1936）

Contents

Synopsis / xv
Acknowledgements / xvi
About the Translators / xvii
Preface to Twenty-Five Poems by Shao Xunmei / xxi

Part One: Heaven and May in 1927 / 1

Heaven Poems /2
0. Prelude /3
1. Heaven / 5
2. Sister Hua Mulan / 20
3. Hair / 46
4. Narcissus / 49
5. A Poem / 51
6. I Have to Be a Contented Insect / 53
7. Complete Recovery / 57
8. Sappho / 59
9. The Third Day of Floating on the Sea / 63
10. Troubled / 65
11. A Sonnet / 67
12. Love / 69
13. The Poet and Jesus / 71
14. A Little Candle / 73

May Poems / 77
15. Song of Love / 78
16. Tomorrow / 80
17. Love / 82
18. Horror / 84
19. Spring / 86
20. Summer / 88
21. Flower / 90
22. May / 94
23. To Sappho / 96
24. To Swinburne / 98
25. I Cannot Stand / 100
26. Come On / 102
27. Monologue of Love / 104
28. Ex Dono Dei / 106
29. A Virgin Man Handling Women / 108
30. Anch'io Sono Pittore! / 110
31. Decadent Love / 114
32. Under the Sunrise Building / 116

Part Two: Twenty-Five Poems in 1936 / 118

1. To a Poet / 119
2. Xunmei's Dream / 121
3. Woman / 125
4. A Little Poem / 127
5. Seasons / 129
6. Voice / 131
7. Nature's Command / 140
8. Heaven and Earth / 144

CONTENTS

9. Undisputed Faith / 146
10. Self / 150
11. Whom Do You Take Me For? / 152
12. Peony / 154
13. In the Eye of a Traveller / 156
14. I Dare Not Go to Heaven / 158
15. Lines of Verse Never Imagined / 160
16. The Voice Sent by the Wind / 162
17. If I Were Also Like an Immortal / 166
18. Green Dies from the Banana / 168
19. A Dead Chinese Lute / 170
20. Serpent / 172
21. Love Looted / 174
22. On the Top of Zijinshan / 176
23. Come down to the Countryside / 178
24. An Old Tree of Two Hundred Years / 180
25. The Newly-Wedded Bride / 184

Appendix A: Shao Xunmei's Translated Poems / 188
1. Worry by Tu Fu / 188
2. The Butterfly's Love by Li Ching-Tsau / 189
3. A Poem by Su Tung-Po / 190
4. Magnolia Flower by Yan Shu / 191

Appendix B: A Chinese Swinburne: Shao Xunmei's Life and Art / 192

Works Cited / 194

目錄

作者自序　　　　／*xxxvii*

第一部分：《天堂與五月》（1927）　／1

天堂之什　　　／2
0. 序曲　　　　　／4
1. 天堂　　　　　／12
2. 花姊姊　　　　／33
3. 頭髮　　　　　／48
4. 水仙嚇　　　　／50
5. 一首詩　　　　／52
6. 我只得也像一隻知足的小蟲　／55
7. 病癒　　　　　／58
8. 莎茀　　　　　／61
9. 漂浮在海上的第三天　／64
10. 憂愁　　　　　／66
11. 十四行詩　　　／68
12. 愛　　　　　　／70
13. 詩人與耶穌　　　　／72
14. 小燭　　　　　／75

五月之什　　　／77
15. 戀歌　　　　　／79
16. 明天　　　　　／81
17. 愛　　　　　　／83
18. 恐怖　　　　　／85
19. 春　　　　　　／87

CONTENTS

20. 夏　　　　　　／ 89
21. 花　　　　　　／ 92
22. 五月　　　　　／ 95
23. 致莎茀　　　　／ 97
24. 致史文朋　　　／ 99
25. 我忍不住了　　／ 101
26. 來吧　　　　　／ 103
27. 愛的叮囑　　　／ 105
28. 恩賜　　　　　／ 107
29. 童男的處女　　／ 109
30. 我也是畫家　　／ 112
31. 穨加蕩的愛　　／ 115
32. 日昇樓下　　　／ 117

第二部分：《詩二十五首》（1936）　／ 118

1. 贈一詩人　　　／ 120
2. 洵美的夢　　　／ 123
3. 女人　　　　　／ 126
4. 一首小詩　　　／ 128
5. 季候　　　　　／ 130
6. 聲音　　　　　／ 136
7. 自然的命令　　／ 142
8. 天和地　　　　／ 145
9. 不變的信念　　／ 148
10. 自己　　　　　／ 151
11. 你以為我是什麼人？　／ 153
12. 牡丹　　　　　／ 155
13. 出門人的眼睛　／ 157
14. 我不敢上天　　／ 159

xiii

15. 永遠想不到的詩句　　　/ 161
16. 風吹來的聲音　　　　　/ 164
17. 假如我也和神仙一樣　　/ 167
18. 綠逃去了芭蕉　　　　　/ 169
19. 死了的琵琶　　　/ 171
20. 蛇　　　　/ 173
21. 情賊　　　/ 175
22. 在紫金山　　　/ 177
23. 到鄉下來　　　/ 179
24. 二百年的老樹　　　/ 182
25. 新嫁娘　　　/ 186

附錄A：邵洵美的英譯詩　　/ 188
1. 春望（杜甫）　　　/ 188
2. 蝶戀花（李清照）　　　/ 189
3. 吉祥寺賞牡丹（蘇東坡）　　　/ 190
4. 木蘭花（晏殊）　　　/ 191

附錄B：中國的史文朋：邵洵美的人生與藝術　　/ 192

Synopsis

Shao Xunmei (1906-68) was an entre-guerre poet from a wealthy Shanghai family who fell under the spell of European poets such as Swinburne, Sappho and the French Symbolists while studying at Cambridge. Back in his hometown, he led a group of Western-inspired writers and artists who wanted to reinvigorate their decrepit country with Western cultural energy, mainly as represented by the *fin-de-siecle* and Modernism. In this respect, Shao's coterie was just one of many intellectual and literary groups competing in Shanghai during the Nationalist Decade. Shao poured all his fortune into his publishing company and magazines, but never became financially successful. He nonetheless lived a colorful life as an East-West cultural hybrid, wearing a traditional scholar's gown with English brogues while juggling an affair with American writer Emily Hahn and being married to a society beauty. The Japanese occupation of Shanghai and the Communist takeover ended Shao's poetic career, and he died in poverty during the Cultural Revolution.

Our translation of Shao's two volumes of poetry reveals both his influence by Swinburne and Verlaine, as well as his unique personal touch. As with any such project, we have striven to create poems that stand on their own in English while remaining faithful to the original. Shao not only combined East and West in his life and art, but also turned his life into his art and vice-versa; we have rendered this in our translation also. At a time of intense cross-cultural scrutiny, especially between Europe and Asia, our translation is a valuable contribution to understanding hybrid creativity.

Acknowledgements

The translators would like to thank Shandong University of Technology for its publishing grant for this book and President Lu Chuanyi, and Professor Wang Xuezhen, Professor Wu Zongjie and Professor Li Jing who went over our grant proposal and offered valuable comments. Our thanks are also extended to Professor Wang Dewei (Harvard University), Professor Chen Zishan (Eastern China Normal University) and Dr. Chen Jun (Peking University), Wanyan Shaoyuan and Ms. Yang Yingzi (Shanghai Bookstore Publishing House) whose assistance was invaluable in preparing the manuscript and the copyright respectively. I would also like to acknowledge Ms. Shao Xiaohong's edition, *Flower-like Evil,* a collection of her father, Shao Xunmei's poems in 2008 which is our original text for the translation.

Acknowledgements are also made to Mr. Tom Lee and Mr. Shawn Ye and Homa & Sekey Books for their unflagging assistance and advice on the text arrangement.

Jicheng Sun & Hal Swindall
February 14, 2016

About the Translators

Jicheng Sun Biography

I was born in Shandong, China in 1970. I went to Shandong Normal University in Jinan in 1988 majoring in English. In 1992, I was an English teacher in Shandong University of Technology from 1992 to 1995. In 1996, I went to Shandong University for my MA study in American literature. In 1999, I worked as a sport news translator and editor for Reuters in Jinan TV Station and in 2000 I went back to Shandong University of Technology for teaching English and translation.

In 2001 I entered the English Department, Peking University for my doctorial study. I have spent more than ten years (2001-2010) in my dissertation entitled as *Christianity in China with the Focus on the Translating History of Christian Holy Names in*

China. During my study, I also translated some books by William Edgar Geil (2008) and Robert Birnbaum (2006) and published several essays about D.H. Lawrence and Shao Xunmei.

In 2003, I worked as an exchange scholar in Stockholm University with supervision by Prof. Torbjorn Loden, Sweden. My project was about the European missionaries to China in 19th century.

My research fields are literary translation, missionary study and comparative culture. My current project is co-translating the Selected Poems of Crescent Moon School with Dr. Harold Swindall. I am now an associate professor of English in Shandong University of Technology, Shandong, China. My email is sunjicheng@hotmail.com and jichengsun@pku.edu.cn.

Hal Swindall Biography

I was born in the Bay Area of California in 1963, and spent my early childhood in northern California. At the age of 10, I moved with my family to the UK for three years while my father pursued doctoral studies at Oxford and Edinburgh. We returned to Riverside in southern California in 1976, and that is where I grew up.

I attended a liberal arts college in New Hampshire for my BA, majoring in Literature, which I received in 1985. Moving back to southern California, I earned my MA in English from Claremont Graduate University in 1986. After that, I moved back to my hometown for doctoral studies in Comparative Literature at the University of California at Riverside. Here, I majored in English and minored in French and Italian. During my years of doctoral studies, I visited France and Italy several times over the summer vacations, having many adventures. My dissertation, which was chaired by the famous American Comparative Literature scholar Jean-Pierre Barricelli, was entitled *The Aesthetic Hero and Fin-de-siecle Critical Fiction*. Its topic was the protagonists in the novels of Walter Pater, JK Huysmans, George Moore, Oscar Wilde and Gabriele d'Annunzio, as well as their art criticism. At present, I am trying to prepare it for publication.

After receiving my PhD in 1994, I decided to go to China to teach, and this move turned into a life-changing career decision. I spent three years in China at two key universities, teaching mainly writing and literature to undergraduates and graduates. At Shandong University in 1995, one of my graduate students was Sean Sun, my co-author for this project on Shao Xunmei, in whom I became interested during that time. Since leaving China, I have taught in Korea, Taiwan and Malaysia. Recently I taught as a professor of English on the Department of Global Studies at Pusan National University in Korea.

Besides my interests in late nineteenth-century Europe and its echo in 1930s Shanghai, I am interested in nineteenth-century art, especially the forgotten Victorian architect and designer Owen Jones; languages, particularly French and Italian but also Mandarin; religious Daoism in China and its temples, many of which I have visited; and amateur travel writing.

My current project on Shao Xunmei with Sean Sun involves the first ever translation into English of *Paradise and May*, his first volume of verse in 1927. We plan to co-translate several of his volumes in the future.

Preface to *Twenty-Five Poems*

I am a little bit embarrassed to select twenty-five poems from my past ten years' writing for the coming publication. From the aspect of its quantity, this collection is too small to form a book. I spent a very limited time in writing because I have many interests to take care of, and also like to poke my nose into others' business; as a result, most of my time has been occupied by non-writing matters, and most of my goodwill endeavors have not been appreciated; until today, I still have no courage to retreat from my busy life. Sometimes, I even doubt if I have the gift of writing poems.

I never expressed my disappointment with the new poetry (also called new verse or modern Chinese poetry); it is true that there is always a lack of critics in the literary world who give moral support[1] to it; thus, without self-knowledge, some poets believe that they are misunderstood by the public, and others think they are treasures which have not been recognized. I have never held such illusions. Whenever I complete a poem, I feel greatly satisfied when my wife likes it, and I will feel happier when some good friends give me unexpected compliments. I never believed in the legend of a poem being passed on for many generations, and being read by many.

I have written new poems for fifteen long years, and I suppose that I am very serious in my creation. For fifteen years, I have worked as busily as Don Quixote, and could not devote myself to serve the muse of poetry wholeheartedly, but I have

---

[1] Shao here uses the Chinese expression *daodede*, meaning moral or spiritual support and guidance.

never stopped my own poetry writing for a minute, which could be regarded as my most proud and most sincere confession.

The reason for the above confession was that the close relationship between the new verse and I remained unknown to the public. In the initial period of my new verse writing, I thought this new verse was my own finding, because I have never received any aspirations from any writers; I even had no chance to read Hu Shi's *A Collection of Attempts*,[1] which I finally read much later. This was because at that time I was in a mission school and read many foreign poems, and then tried to release their meanings in our vernacular language (as one of the children in a traditional family, I didn't know there was a movement of Written Vernacular Chinese). Then when a classmate lent me a newspaper supplement in Shanghai known as *A Study Lamp*,[2] I came to know this kind of verse writing had involved the efforts of many predecessors. Again by another classmate's introduction, I bought a copy of the magazine of *Creation*,[3] (*Chuangzao*), which helped me to believe more in my determination to have my own faith in the new verse. Yet up to then I had no chance to know anything about its greatness,

---

[1] Hu Shi (1891-1962) was a Chinese philosopher, essayist and diplomat. Hu is widely recognized today as a key contributor to Chinese liberalism and language reform in his advocacy for the use of written vernacular Chinese (the *baihua* literary movement) that started in 1919. Hu's book's title is *Changshiji (A Collection of Attempts)* in Chinese.

[2] *Xuedeng* in Chinese was the supplement to *China Times* (Shishixinbao) in Shanghai. It was founded in March 4, 1918, and was one of most influential supplements.

[3] This was called *Chuangzao* in Chinese, and was the journal of a major *Baihua* school, Chuangzaoshe (The Creation Society), which was founded and led by Guo Moruo, Cheng Fangwu and others in Japan in July, 1921, and was forced to close in February, 1922.

so even Mr. Xu Zhimo's name[1] didn't reach my ears. It seems funny that I did not know anything at that time about the common sense in the new verse writing, and also lucky in keeping me from being influenced by any writers in that field.

Mentioning these experiences, I, of course, am not saying that a poet should not be influenced and impacted by any others; I just intend to remind my readers not to compare my poetry with others'--otherwise, they will be lost. Concerning the influences I have since received in my own writing of the new verse, the most obvious is that of foreign poems, which you can find everywhere in my works. These foreign influences are neither a glory nor a shame, but an inevitable phenomenon, because I lived with them day and night. Of course one would catch some of their breath in reading these foreign lines. I also deliberately imitated their rules and compositional forms. But my attitude was not pedantic. I did not want to introduce new shackles to the writing of poetry; on the contrary, I wanted to find a new order for the new verse.

I thought Hu Shi and his followers were advocating writing articles and poems in the vernacular language, but their achievements were mainly in culture, while in literature they were just suggesting some hints. I believe that the essential condition of any literature is its techniques of diction. This was the essential tool for literary writers; but besides translating classical into modern Chinese, Hu Shi did not give us some new techniques. This situation was changed by Xu Zhimo, who was himself a poet, so it was a pity that he only made use of

---

[1] Xu Zhimo (1897-1931) was one of the most renowned romantic poets of 20th-century Chinese literature, and is known for his promotion of modern Chinese poetry, which has made tremendous contributions to modern Chinese literature.

these new techniques as his own decoration, making it difficult for him to declare them open for everyone to enjoy. Wen Yiduo[1] was a scholar of poetics, but he only introduced some skills from some foreign poetic forms. Liu Wuji[2], Zhu Xiang[3] and others introduced foreign poetic forms on a large scale, but because their poems were just imitations of foreign ones, they were made fun of as Western chains on Chinese writing. That said, of course, we apparently misunderstood the purpose of these scholars, but if their foreign skills had been completely accepted, people would probably have misinterpreted them. Among them, Sun Dayu[4] was the one who successfully introduced foreign skills into his own poems. Sun understood them thoroughly, and practiced them openly, and thus achieved the greatest effect upon his readers; once "The Portrayal of Self" was published in the magazine *Poetry*, it was imitated by young poets for many years. Soon after, Dai Wangshu[5] brought his grand performance to the new verse writing, and then it

---

[1] Wen Yiduo (1899-1946) was a famous poet of the New Crescent Society and studied and taught in Tsinghua University. In 1922, his first collection of poetry, *Hongzhu* (Red Candle), was published. In 1928, his second collection, *Sishui* (Dead Water), was published. In 1928, he joined the Crescent Moon Society and wrote essays on poetry, mostly stressing that poetry should have "formal properties".

[2] Liu Wuji (1907-2002) was a famous poet and scholar. He graduated from Tsinghua University in 1927 and got a PhD from Yale University in 1931. In 1931, he founded *Literature Magazine* with other friends.

[3] Zhu Xiang (1904-1933) was a famous poet of the Crescent School. His best poem collections are *Summer* (1925) and *Stone Gate Collection* (1934). He was regarded as one of the most important poets in the New Verse Movement.

[4] Sun Dayu (1905-1997) was a poet of the Crescent School and a translator and a Shakespeare scholar. He studies in Tsinghua University in 1922 and Yale University during 1928-1930.

[5] Dai Wangshu (1905-1950) was a famous poet of modern symbolism. One of his famous poems is "A Lane in the Rain".

became a fashion.

Of course, only new techniques could not be enough for creating good new verses. We all know that besides his skills in the new verse writing, Sun Dayu was noted for his heroic spirit, while Dai Wangshu was good at describing his delicate emotions with his skills, which makes him impossible to imitate. From this, we can see that new images are more important than new techniques for the writing of new verse. Hu Shi has neither new techniques nor new images, so he was the leader of the new culture, rather than the head of the new verse movement. So when we are talking about the new verse, we had better not take Hu Shi too seriously (though his other accomplishments are worthy of our serious study). Of course, I do not mean to say that the relationship between Hu Shi and the new poetry can be wiped out completely. But now that the new verse has developed its techniques in a constructive way, Hu's position in art is apparently not so important. New verse in China is no longer the simple intra-lingual translation of the classical Chinese poetry into the vernacular; it is no longer prose which is written line by line. As long as we see the latest new verses by Sun Dayu, Bian Zhilin[1] and others, we will realize these changes are definite.

Every age has its own rhyme, and every age has its own form of new verse which expresses it. And now the performance of this new rhyme has appeared in Sun Dayu and Bian Zhilin's greatest achievements. While the former caught hold

---

[1] Bian Zhilin (1910-2000) was a 20th-century Chinese poet, translator and literature researcher. Bian's poems were related to the New Crescent School, which advocated modern metrical poetry, but his style was closer to the Chinese symbolists.

of the complexity of mechanical civilization, and the latter saw through the loneliness of spiritual culture, both of them identified the color of each word as well as its weight; they found out the time and distance in each sentence. Both put the looks and sounds of an era into their new poems; at the same time, they described a spirited life which follows the universe and develops with it. This technique cannot be understood by Hu Shi, because these techniques have reached the most special state of poetry writing, which cannot easily understood by people with too much common sense.

The above has simply stated that the new poetry has developed into a new phase at a new level, and has also explained why the new poetry in recent years appeared after a period of silence; in fact, the new poets are spending much of their efforts exercising their new techniques in verse writing so as to achieve a greater mature performance. Now let me tell you briefly about my own story of new verse writing.

As a certain literary critic, Harold Nicolson[1], said: "The motivation of all literary movements is to rebel against the inherent theory of the former generation." China's New Culture Movement is also out to damage the traditional ones. It wants to bring down the old moral codes, overthrow classical Chinese and change the metrics rules of traditional poetry .... Though Hu Shi later constructed some literary theory, the sources for his construction are still rebellious. Therefore, his theory of poetry and examples remain the same as when he called on his "vernacular free verse." It is a source of pride and also a stroke

---

[1] Harold Nicolson (1886-1968) published a biography of French poet *Paul Verlaine* in 1921, and studies of other literary figures such as Tennyson, Byron, Swinburne and Sainte-Beuve.

of luck for me not to have been involved with that movement simply because of my small age; I started to write my new verse out of my own motivation, which came from my failure when I translated foreign poems in terms of traditional Chinese poetry, and also from my inspiration in reading vernacular novels in dialects.

My first creation in the new verse was a prose poem, entitled "On February 14," which was published in *Women's Magazine* [*Funuzazhi*] by the Commercial Press. I have also written many small poems which have been thought as having influenced by the popular Japanese haiku style; in fact, speaking ashamedly, they are just my versions and translations of famous British poems, though some of them have combined original creation as well as trifling inspiration. When they were published, some of my friends began to bring me Zhou Zuoren[1] and Bing Xin's[2] poems for comparison; what a coincidence that between our poems I received some unexpected lessons, and I hated this tricky corruption in my writing and started to explore it more seriously.

Before leaving for Europe, I got some gifts from my friend, including copies of *The Goddess* (*Nushen*) and *Winter Night* (*Dongye*).[3] In reading, I felt a new strength creeping from

---

[1] Zhou Zuoren (1885-1967) was a Chinese writer, primarily known as an essayist and a translator. Writing essays in vernacular Chinese for the influential magazine *La Jeunesse*, Zhou was a key figure in the May Fourth Movement. He was an advocate of literary reform.

[2] Bing Xin (1900-1999) was the pen name of Xie Wanying, who was one of the most prolific Chinese writers of the 20th century. Many of her works were written for young readers.

[3] *The Goddess* (*Nushen*) was the first collected poems of Guo Moruo (1892-1978), published in 1921 and sometimes was regarded as the first influential

these books, but I disliked how they were too careless and lax. In Naples, I was fascinated by a mural of the Greek female poet Sappho in the museum. I was so amazed by this goddess that I happened to find an English copy of her poetry, and I guessed there was some similarity between Chinese classical verse and hers in many places. With my tender, weak soul, I thought this was a great discovery. By this time, Xu Dishan[1] was in Oxford, and I wrote him a letter to discuss this groundless "discovery" with him. I have forgotten what Xu had said in his reply, though it was probably not lacking in praise and encouragement. Afterwards, I embraced a dream of creating a new poetic form, and then wrote a lot of new poems with the borrowed style of Sappho, among which one poem was published in a collection called *Heaven and May*. In this collection, there are various kinds of poetic styles that now look very childish, and whenever people mention them, I will blush.

My exploration in the new verse writing seemed strange. I happened to find Sappho, and from her I found her admirer, Swinburne, and from Swinburne I met the Pre-Raphaelites, and then from them I accessed Baudelaire and Verlaine. During this period, I worked on how to choose gorgeous words, novel phrases and clangorous syllables, and neglected how the more important thing in poetry is the image. Later on, I became an intimate of Xu Zhimo, but from him I only got ex-

---

book of new poetry in China. *Winter Night (Dongye, 1922)* was a collected poems of Yu Pingbo (1900-1990), an essayist, poet, historian, Redologist, and critic.

[1] Xu Dishan (1894-1941) was a Chinese author, translator and folklorist. He was best known for his Chinese novels that focus on the people of the southern provinces of China and Southeast Asia.

cessive encouragement and praise. Also in this period, I published my first poetry collection, *Flower-like Evil*. I once heard that Xu Zhimo said behind my back to a friend: "There is a new poet in China who is 100 percent Verlaine." If he had said these words to me in person, I would have never realized my mistakes as late as in the last five years.

Maybe this exploration is always the touchstone for every poet, to which he inevitably has been tempted, because at first he has been moved by the poetry he reads, often by its shallow philosophy in one line or two, or touched by sentimental words or praises of lust. Writing poetry for the first time must be cheeky imitation. Further is the temptation of rhetoric; further still is intoxication with tones. I hold that the golden rule of poetics is what Swinburne once said: "I don't have to determine the form of poetry by metrical rules; I can decide it with my ears." And as William Morris[1] said: "I don't believe in any inspiration; I only know that there are skills." So for the past five years, my poems were mostly carved most delicately; in addition to the satisfaction of people's eyes and ears, they have only their literal meanings.

This "young show-off" has changed since I completed my poem "Xunmei's Dream." At the same time, I began to work on the texture of my new verse. The poem "Woman" is the first attempt of mine in this direction. Its form is neat quatrains, of which each stanza has the same number of words

---

[1] William Morris (1834-1896) was a prolific writer of poetry, fiction, essays, and translations of ancient and medieval texts. Morris began publishing poetry and short stories in 1856 through the *Oxford and Cambridge Magazine,* which he founded with his friends and financed while at university. "The Haystack in the Floods" in his first volume, *The Defence of Guenevere and Other Poems* (1858), is probably now one of his better-known poems.

with different rhymes. To write this poem is to describe the feeling of pleasantness and surprise, and to show that a person can have two kinds of feelings at the same time. The first stanza is about both respect and fear, and its tone sounds more suppressed; the second stanza is about being suspicion and happiness, and its tone sounds more magnified. Concerning its rhetorical effect, metrical changes and various images, I intended to make some reconciliation among them.

After the poem "Woman," I also completed others, such as "Voice," "Nature's Command," "Heaven and Earth" and "Undisputed Faith." "Voice" and "Nature's Command" are my experiments in pentameter blank verse; "Heaven and Earth" is my trial with the Western sonnet; and "Undisputed Faith" is my attempt in tetrameter blank verse. But my attempts in metrical changes were serious in essence, and not for the sake of their formal changes. For example, the characteristics of pentameter blank verse extend the power of the situation, which can thus have more natural and more complex changes; though it also has a disruption, but its artistic tone is coherent; even if the reader takes a break in his reading, or even stops reading for a few days, when he wants to read on, the spirit in the poem can still be resumed. Just as a boat sails on the water, even though the river's course appears sometimes straight, sometimes bending, sometimes wide, sometimes narrow, sometimes crossing a little tunnel or gorge, as long as it follows the course of the flow, in the end it will run into the sea after its flowing of hundreds or thousands miles. But its life is as constant as a spider's thread, which even a storm cannot separate or damage. In long poems, this metrical arrangement will not make the reader feel it is so long; to appreciate it, of course, demands a healthy mind, while a mind split or distracted by some stimulus cannot enjoy its beauty, and it can only make such readers feel weak and strange. Tetrameter blank verse has little change in its metrical methods, because if it is too long, it will be monotonous, but the aesthetic feeling is more friendly, more simple, more suitable for the naive artistic situation.

The sonnet is the most complete and the most refined poetic form among foreign genres, and is just like China's *jueju*,[1] which are like the old saying that "A sparrow may be small, but it has all the vital organs." One is itself a complete life and a whole world. The sonnet form is chiefly appreciated for recording the most pure emotion in an artistic situation. It has more changes than China's *jueju*, and can be used to practice new skills and attain very good results in new verse writing. Of course, I don't advise people to find out what range of subject matter can be written in sonnets, but I do suggest that the order of words is a must in sonnet writing. I always trust Samuel Taylor Coleridge's credo in his own poetry writing: "Poetry is the best words in their best order."

I feel a real poet must have his own style of "the best order." Fixed rules will not help him, but also will not hinder him. Thus, I believe that a metrical pattern is not a limitation for a poet to follow, but a guide for the reader to understand his poems; the arrangement of words and the patterns of rhyme make poems as convenient as possible for people to appreciate. At the same time, the patterns of tones, the numbers of words and the rhymes of lines in traditional Chinese poems

---

[1] *Jueju* were traditional Chinese quatrains which grew popular among Chinese poets in the Tang Dynasty (618-907), although traceable to earlier origins. The five-syllable form is called *wujue* and the seven-syllable form *qijue*.

play the same effect on readers. Different lines and foot meters are foreign, and they are new techniques for Chinese; therefore, the new verse writing possesses at least these two techniques. Also, the patterns of tones in Chinese traditional poems are real shackles, so we have to abolish them.

"Perfection of form is the greatest virtue," said Theophile Gautier.[1] Perfect form is what I pursue in my poetry. But perfect form, in my opinion, is not only what is referred to as even and tidy; a neat form is sometimes absolutely ugly. Form can be perfect only if it is in harmony with the character of poetry itself.

Concerning the nature of poetry and its subject matter, I also have a few ideas to share, so let me sum up my viewpoint so as to end this preamble.

Generally, people who don't like the new verse say that it is difficult to understand, and recently even Hu Shi and Liang Shiqiu[2] have repeatedly said that the new verse should be clearly understandable. The former offers a general criticism

---

[1] Theophile Gautier (1811-1872) was a French poet, novelist and critic generally credited with launching the art for art's sake movement with his preface to his novel *Mademoiselle de Maupin* (1835). He was a friend of Charles Baudelaire and was greatly admired by Swinburne, who wrote essays introducing him to the British reading public.

[2] Liang Shiqiu (1903-1987) was a renowned educator, writer, translator, literary theorist and lexicographer. He was educated at Tsinghua College in Beijing from 1915 to 1923. He went on to study at Colorado College and later pursued his graduate studies at Harvard and Columbia Universities. At Harvard, he studied literary criticism under Irving Babbitt, whose New Humanism helped shape his conservative literary tenets. After his return to China in 1926, he began a long career as a professor of English at several universities, including Peking University, Tsingtao University, and Jinan University. He also served as the editor of a succession of literary supplements and periodicals, including the famous *Crescent Moon Monthly* (1928–1933).

that obviously is irresponsible and stubborn, and probably neither has ever read new verse; the latter has always had difficulty explaining the real reasons behind their statements. The present situation of the new verse, except for a few special talents, appears to have some common maladies. But the solutions given by Hu Shi and Liang Shiqiu can only be regarded as temporary healing prescriptions, not as permanent remedies.

I think that real poetry is not understood clearly. E. M. W. Tillyard[1], a modern British critic, once said in his book *Poetry Direct and Oblique* (Chatto & Windus, 1959): "In all poems there are always some twists and turns, and we have never had some oblique poems." But such comments are based on poems' convenience for analysis, and he then divides them into two kinds: the "direct" and the "oblique." Let me now explain this kind of compromise of his classification in my own words. Actually, this definition of a "direct poem" barely holds any water; once a poem is really direct in itself, it will enter the field of prose. So here the so-called "direct poem" can only be explained as a "descriptive" one. Of course, this descriptive type of poem can be classified into lyric, scenery description, narrative and philosophical poetry, but they can be regarded as "poems" by specification, and their adjectives are used as the "interpretation of metaphor." Once this kind of adjective turns into the word "symbol," the poem will have its twists and turns. To explain what the role of a symbol is, I'm afraid that it will need a

---

[1] Eustace Mandeville Wetenhall Tillyard (1889-1962) was a British classical scholar and literary scholar. He was a Fellow in English (1926–1959) at Jesus College, later becoming Master (1945–1959). He is known mainly for his book *The Elizabethan World Picture* (1942), as background to Elizabethan literature, particularly Shakespeare, and for his *John Milton* (1946).

book to do it: roughly, the descriptive metaphor is a temporary symbol, and the permanent symbol is described and interpreted forever; and all great poems always have a permanent symbol. But when a poem can be explained in terms of description and parables, it has also become oblique in itself.

Therefore, if the poem intends to be absolutely direct and clear, it has become prose. But it is not easy to appreciate a poem of obliquity; in doing so, the reader needs to read it sincerely: he must have the determination to taste the joy of this poem. Average readers will wince at these difficulties. So considering the fate of the new poetry, we may wish to reduce its obliquity, and step by step guide its readers on the road to its understanding. Otherwise, they may be frightened and never approach it; at the same time, we can also stop their criticisms of minor aspects of the new verse so as not to waste our breath. When we actually talk about the achievements of most of the new verse, their results are very naive, and far from being direct or oblique at all. So what we have to deal with is not the "oblique poem," which is the real one, but usually the "falsely oblique poem," which generally does not make a good word choice which is pretentious, naive and poor.

The new poetic issue worth discussing is that of its subject matter. The transformation of original form and the development of the thematic change are also inevitable phenomena. We will use the most obvious example to illustrate the above, i.e., before the invasion of modern civilization, there were all sorts of restrictions on travel; except for officials of high rank being assigned to new posts or businessmen, people always stayed in their hometowns, where they saw the natural scenery and felt the quietness of nature. Those who enjoyed travelling would take with them dried food and good wine while roaming about, but what they contacted was also the beauty of the landscape, the innocent birds and animals; they wrote their poetry in such an atmosphere, and their themes were lofty.

But now, the city's prosperity has seduced all the innocent hearts of the field, and material civilization has influenced every family, the effect of which is that they can travel from huts to high modern buildings of 20 floors of steel and cement in an hour or two, while their sensual feelings and their pulse beats have become more acute. Writing poetry has become different from the past; if a poet has not changed, he will be made fun of as artificial and contrived, or in a cowardly escape from reality. All descriptive words and abstract nouns have changed their original meanings; the transformation of thematic concerns is a tendency people cannot reverse. Now the poet of new verse encounters a harder task: he is going to create a new vocabulary; he is supposed to have godlike power and technique to make the most disharmonious things blend harmoniously. This might give the impression of some difficulties for readers, who will suspect that the poet writes just for the sake of his own writing. In fact, the poet's mission is to have a Midas touch that adds some new meanings to old things.

As I have said before, "Poetry is a flash in man's records of all human truth." The first carriage in poets' writing train is by no means the locomotive, which is a train's soul; it is also like a picture of the universe, where there is no real understanding at a glance. All in all, it does not matter if we understand a poem or not, but it really matters saying that it is the poet's wild absurdity that make us fail to understand it. To comprehend a really great poet, we should know that he is always willing to undertake his mission to complete the important task of turning all creatures into gold; to get to know a great poet, we should use our devotion to respect him, because in front of a truly great poet, all problems become non-problematic at all.

    These are my opinions of the new verse, which is my faith, and is also my confession. Of course, I dare not hope that you will use the same measure to measure my poetry; but I believe that a serious work will never be reduced in seriousness due to the exaggeration of chosen measures.

Shao Xunmei
April 1, 1936

作者自序
(《詩二十五首》自序)

十年的詩只有二十五首可以勉強見得來人。從數量方面說，真是寒酸得可憐。我的興趣多，喜管閒事；結果是自己吃了虧，人家還是不願意；寫文章的時間大部分讓別種東西占去，到今天仍沒有退縮的勇氣；有時候簡直懷疑自己和詩的緣分。

我對於新詩從沒有表示過失望，文壇上缺少批評家來給予一種"道德的協助"是事實；無自知之明的便相信自己受了委屈，以為自己是一件未被人發現的寶貝。我從沒有過這種幻想，寫成一首詩，只要老婆看了說好，已是十分快樂；假使熟朋友再稱讚幾句，更是意外的收穫；千古留名，萬人爭誦，那種故事，我是當作神話看的。

我寫新詩已有十五年以上的歷史，自信是十二分的認真；十五年來雖然因了幹著吉訶德先生式的工作，以致不能一心一意去侍奉詩神，可是龕前的供養卻從沒有分秒的間斷，這是我最誠懇最驕傲的自白。

原因是我和新詩關係的密切是任何人所不知道的。最初的時期尚以為是自己的發現，我寫新詩從沒有受誰的啟示，即連胡適之的《嘗試集》也還是過後才見到的。當時是因為在教會學校裏讀到許多外國詩，便用通俗語言來試釋，(作為一個舊家庭的子弟，他並沒有知道世上有所謂白話文運動。)到後來一位同學借給了我一份《學燈》，才知道這類工作正有許多前輩在努力。又由另一位同學的介紹，買到了本《創造》，於是更堅決了自己的信仰；但是新詩人中最偉大的徐志摩，連名字都沒有聽到。當時常識的缺乏，現在想想真好笑；不過也便是為了如此，所以我的作品未曾受到過什麼壞影響。

我講這些話，當然並不是說一個詩人不應受到任何種的薰陶與影響；我只是要讀我的詩的人知道，假使把我的詩去和人家的詩比較，他是會迷途的。

我也並不是說我沒有受到過任何種的薰陶與影響，外國詩的蹤跡在我的字句裏是隨處可以尋得的。這個不是榮耀，也不是羞恥，這是必然的現象，一天到晚和他們在一起，你當然會沾染到一些他們的氣息。我也曾故意地去摹仿過他們的格律，但是我的態度不是迂腐的，我決不想介紹一個新桎梏，我是要發現一種新秩序。

　　我以為胡適之等雖然提倡了用白話寫文章寫詩，但他們的成就是文化上的；在文學上，他們不過是盡了提示的責任。我相信文學的根本條件是"文字的技巧"，這原是文學者絕對不能缺少的工具；但是他們除了把文言譯成白話以外，並沒有給我們看過一些新技巧。這番工作到了徐志摩手裏，才有了一些眉目，可惜他自己也是詩人，於是這些新技巧便變了他自己的裝飾，而不容易叫大家公開地享受。聞一多是一位詩藝的學者，但他介紹的外國技巧都偏重在形式方面。柳無忌、朱湘等也曾大規模地把外國詩的形式介紹到中國來，但因為是十足的摹仿，於是被人譏為西洋的鐐銬。說這種話的當然太不瞭解學者的苦心，不過不徹底的全盤接收是難免會引起人家誤會的。孫大雨是從外國帶了另一種新技巧來的人，他透徹，明顯，所以效力大；《自己的寫照》在《詩刊》登載出來以後，一時便來了許多青年詩人的仿製。不久戴望舒又有他巧妙的表現，立刻成了一種風氣。

　　當然，光有新技巧也不夠。我們知道孫大雨在技巧以外還有他雄樸的氣概，戴望舒在技巧以外還有他深致的情緒，摹仿他們的人於是始終望塵莫及。從這裏，我們可以明白，有了新技巧還要有新意象，胡適之卻一樣也沒有，因此他只是新文化的領袖而不是新詩的元首。

　　所以我們要談新詩，最好先把胡適之來冷淡（他自身的成就是另外一件事情）。我當然並不是說他和新詩的歷史關係可以完全抹殺，但是當新詩的技巧已經進步到有建設的意義的現在，他在藝術上的地位顯然是不重要的了。

　　新詩已不再是由文言詩譯成的白話詩，新詩已不再是分行寫的散文，我們只要一看孫大雨、卞之琳等的近作便可以確信。

每一個時代有每一個時代的韻節，每一個時代又總有一種新詩去表現這種新的韻節。而表現這種新的韻節便是孫大雨、卞之琳等最大的成就。前者捉住了機械文明的複雜，後者看透了精神文化的寂寞；他們確定了每一個字的顏色與分量，他們發現了每一個句斷的時間與距離。他們把這一個時代的相貌與聲音收在詩裏，同時又有活潑的生命會跟著宇宙一同滋長。這種技巧是為胡適之等所不能瞭解的；因為他們已達到了詩的最特殊的境界，盡有豐富的常識還是不容易去理會。

上面是簡單地說明新詩已發展到了什麼程度；同時也解釋新詩在近年來雖然外表上有過一時期的沉默，事實上新詩人是無時無刻不在努力鍛煉他們的技巧，以求一個偉大成熟的表現。下面讓我約略說一說我自己的詩。

英國文學批評家尼古爾生說過："一切文學運動的動機都是要反叛他們前代的故有的理論。"中國的新文化運動也是破壞的，他們要打倒舊禮教，打倒文言，打倒舊詩的格律……雖然胡適之後來有過建設文學的理論，但是他的根據仍舊是"反面的"。所以他的新詩理論與例子到了"白話自由詩"便中止了。我所引為驕傲而慶倖的便是當時我的年齡小沒有加入他們的運動；我的寫新詩便幾乎完全是由自己發動的；我一方面因為舊體詩翻譯外國詩失敗，一方面因為常讀舊式方言小說而有得到了白話的啟示。

我第一次的新詩創作卻是首散文詩，題為《二月十四日》，登在某年某月商務印書館出版的《婦女雜誌》裏。我還有許多小詩，人家看了或者會以為受著當時流行的日本俳句式小詩的影響；事實上，說來慚愧，他們都是些英國名詩的節譯或改作，間或有自己的創制，也無非是些瑣碎的靈感。他們在一個不相干的地方發表出來以後，方才有朋友拿了周作人、冰心等的詩給我看；偶然的巧合竟給了我一個意外的教訓，我從此厭惡這種貪易取巧的工作而開始更嚴重的探求。

動身到歐洲以前，有人送我一本《女神》，一本《冬夜》，我感覺到一種新的力量在蠕動，但是嫌他們的草率與散漫。在意大利的拿波裏上了岸，博物院裏一張壁畫的殘片使我驚異於希臘女詩人莎茀的神麗，輾轉覓到了一部她的全詩的英譯；又從她的詩格裏，猜想到許多地方有和中國舊體詩形似處，嫩弱的靈魂以為這是個偉大的發現。這時候許山在牛津，我竟會寫了封信把這一個毫無根底的意見去和他討論。他回信怎麼說我已忘掉，大概不缺少贊許與鼓勵。過後我便懷抱了個創造新詩格的癡望，當時寫了不少借用"莎茀格"的詩，有一首發表在一本叫做《天堂與五月》的集子裏。這集子裏還有各種詩格的嘗試，現在看來都是幼稚得可憐，人家一提起我便臉紅。

我的詩的行程也真奇怪，從莎茀發見了他的崇拜者史文朋，從史文朋認識了先拉斐爾派的一群，又從他們那裏接觸到波特萊爾、凡爾侖。當時只求豔麗的字眼，新奇的詞句，鏗鏘的音節，竟忽略了更重要的還有詩的意象。後來和徐志摩有了深交，但是從他那裏我只得到過分的獎譽。在這個時期裏我出版了《花一般的罪惡》。聽說徐志摩當時在我的背後對一位朋友說："中國有個新詩人，是一百分的凡爾侖。"這幾句話要是他親口對我說了，我決不會到了五年前方才明白我自己的錯誤。

也許這是每一個寫詩人所必然地要經受的試探，因為我們第一次被詩來感動，每每是為了一兩行淺薄的哲學，或是纏綿的情話，或是肉欲的歌頌。第一次寫詩便一定是一種厚顏的摹仿。再進一步是詞藻的誘惑；再進一步是聲調的沉醉。我當時所認為金科玉律的詩論，便是史文朋所說的："我不用格律來決定詩的形式，我用耳朵來決定"；以及摩理斯所說的："我不相信有什麼靈感，我只知道有技巧"。所以我五年前的詩，大都是雕琢得最精緻的東西；除了給人眼睛及耳朵的滿足以外，便只有字面上所露示的意義。

這種"少壯的炫耀"，寫了《淘美的夢》便盡竭了。同時我便在"肌理"上用工夫。《女人》是第一次的嘗試。形式上是兩段整齊的四行詩，字數前後一樣，韻節卻有變化。這首詩寫又驚又喜的性情，並說一個人同時可以有兩種感覺。前段因為是寫敬重與驚畏，所以抑多於揚；後段因為是寫疑心與快樂，所以揚多於抑；在詞藻上，在韻節上，在意象上，我要求能得到互相貫通的效果。《聲音》、《自然的命令》、《天和地》，以及 Undisputed Faith 等都是《女人》以後的作品。《聲音》和《自然的命令》是"五步無韻詩"的嘗試，《天和地》是"十四行詩"的嘗試，Undisputed Faith 是"四步無韻詩"的嘗試。但是我的格律的嘗試，是性質的，不是形式的。譬如"五步無韻詩"的特點是在能使情境的力量延長，它可以有更自然更複雜的變化；它也有間斷，但氣韻是連貫的，讀的人即使在中間休息一下，甚至擱置幾天，但是當他要繼續讀下去的時候，精神仍舊能會聚。正像是水上行船，那河道有時筆直，有時彎曲，有時寬，有時狹，有時要經過橋洞與山峽；悠長是這條流動的路程，兩端的距離盡使有幾百里幾千里，但是它的生命是一根不斷的蛛絲，狂風暴雨也破壞不得它一分一毫。用這種格律，長詩會覺不到長；去欣賞它當然要有健康的心靈，而希望一剎那的刺激的卻只能怨怪自己的病弱。"四步無韻詩"變化的可能少，太長了會單調，但是它的情致更來得親切，更來得素樸，適宜於更天真的意境。"十四行詩"是外國詩裏最完整最精煉的體裁，正像中國的"絕詩"一樣，"麻雀雖小，五臟俱全"，它自身便是個完全的生命，整個的世界。去記錄一個最純粹的情感的意境，這是最適宜的。它比中國的"絕詩"更多變化，用它來練習新詩的技巧，可以得到極好的成績。我當然不勸人家去就什麼範圍，但是字句的秩序是不可不有的。"詩是最好的字眼在最好的秩序裏。"我始終信任柯勒立治這句話。

我覺得一個真正的詩人一定有他自己的"最好的秩序"。固定的格律不會給他幫助，也不會給他妨礙。所以我們與其說格律是給寫詩人的一種規範，不如說是給讀詩人的一種指點；字句的排列與音韻的佈置，不過是為便利別人去欣賞。舊詩裏的平仄，字數與韻腳，也是這種作用。分行與音尺是外國來的新技巧，所以新詩至少比舊詩要多兩種工具。而舊詩的平仄乃是真正的煉鎖，所以我們把來廢除了。

"形式的完美是最大的德行"，這是高諦藹的話。形式的完美便是我的詩所追求的目的。但是我這裏所謂的形式，並不只指整齊；單獨的形式的整齊有時是絕端醜惡的。只有能與詩的本身的"品性"諧和的方是完美的形式。

關於詩的性質與題材，我也有一些意見；讓我說一說，以結束這篇序文。

大凡不喜歡新詩的都說新詩看不懂，即連胡適之與梁實秋最近也再三說新詩應當要明白清楚，前者那種籠統的批評，顯然是不負責任的固執，他們也許從來就沒有讀過新詩。後者的說話背面有苦衷。新詩的現狀，除了幾個特殊的人材，的確有一種普遍的病象；但是胡適之與梁實秋所給的，只能作為暫時的藥石，而不能作為永久的丹方。我以為詩是根本不會明白清楚的。英國現代批評家諦裏雅在他的《詩的明顯與曲折》一書裏也說過："所有的詩多少總有些曲折的；我們從沒有明顯的詩。"但是他為了要便利評論起見，便把詩分為"明顯的"與"曲折的"兩種。讓我現在也根據了他這一種遷就的分類來解釋。其實"明顯的詩"這一個名目，的確勉強到了極點；一首詩到了真正明顯的時候，它便走進了散文的領域。所以這裏所謂"明顯的詩"只能作為"說明的詩"來解釋。當然抒情詩，寫景詩，敘事詩，說理詩，都可以算是"說明的詩"，但是所用的形容詞至多到了"譬喻"便要為止；一到字眼發生了"象徵的作用"時，詩便曲折了。要說明什麼是"象徵的作用"恐怕非寫一部書不可：大概形容和譬喻是暫時的象徵，象徵則是永久的形容和譬喻；而凡是偉大的詩都有一種永久的象徵性。不過等到一首詩要用形容及譬喻時，它便也已經曲折了，所以詩要絕對明顯，除非寫得和散文一樣。但是要去欣賞一首曲折的詩是不容易的；讀詩的人要有十二分的誠意；他要有品味的決心才能得到理解的享受。平常人每會畏難退縮。所以為整個新詩的命運著想，我們目前不妨減少它的曲折，一步步把讀詩的人引上路來。否則他們會嚇得永遠不敢和它接近；同時我們也可以停止他們的枝節的指摘，以免浪費我們的口舌。其實從大部分的新詩來講，成績是極其幼稚的，根本還談不到明顯與曲折。所以我們要對付的並不是"曲折的詩"，真正的詩，而是一般"假曲折的詩"，一般不會造句或是故弄玄虛的幼稚與拙劣作品。

　　新詩界中還有一個值得討論的是題材問題。原來題材的變換與形式的發展，同樣地是一種必然的現象。我們便用最明顯的例子來說，譬如在現代文明侵入以前，交通有著各種的阻礙，除了出外做官或是經商的，總是勾留在自己的家鄉，所見到的是自然的景色，所感到的是自然的閒靜；即有性好走動的人，帶著美酒乾糧，四處浪遊，所接觸的也無非是山水的秀麗，鳥獸的天真；在這種氛圍裏寫詩，題材自會清高。到了現在，都市的熱鬧誘惑了一切田野的心靈，物質文明的勢力也竄進了每一家門戶，一兩個小時中從茅草屋可以來到二十層的鋼骨水門汀的高廈門前，官能的感受已經更求尖銳，脈搏的跳動已經更來得猛烈；在這種時代裏再寫和往昔一樣的詩句，人家不笑他做作，也要說他是在懦怯地逃避現實了。一切的形容字，抽象名詞，都已更改了他們原來的意義；題材的變換已不是人力所能拒絕。新詩人的手頭便來了個更繁難的工作，他要創造新的字彙；他要有上帝一樣的涵量及手法，使最不調和的東西能和諧地融合。這個也許會給予讀詩的人一個艱難的印象，他們更會疑心到詩人只是為了自己而寫作。其實詩人的使命是"點化"。我以前說過，"詩是曇花一現的真理的盡人力的記載"。詩人所寫的火車龍頭，決不是火車龍頭的機器的組織，乃是火車龍頭的靈魂的系統；正像一幅宇宙的圖畫，沒有慧心，你不能在一瞭眼間領悟這靈機。總之，我們懂不懂是一件事，但是我們決不能因為不懂而說這是詩人的荒蕩。要知一個真正偉大的詩人，他是無時無刻不自己負起去點化全生靈的重任的；去瞭解他，你應當用十二分的虔誠與尊敬，所以在一個真正偉大的詩人面前，一切問題都不成其為問題。

　　這些是我的意見，也是我的信仰，也是我的供狀。我當然不敢希望你們用同一種的衡量來衡量我的詩；但是我相信，一件認

THE VERSE OF SHAO XUNMEI

真的作品也決不會因了衡量的誇張而縮小了自己的尺寸。

邵洵美
二十五年四月一日

Part One: Heaven and May in 1927

第一部分:《天堂與五月》(1927)

Heaven Poems
天堂之什

PART ONE: HEAVEN AND MAY

0. Prelude

I have already known there is an end for everything between heaven and earth;
In the end, the stretch of leaves has broken the silence in the woods.
Whatever sleeps is together with death; but its what if its waking-up at this moment
Turns out to be the seduction of woman's looks, the urge of sensual pleasure and the evil of impulsive obsession?

These wrecked fates, filthy and fallen souls,
Like abandoned skeletons piled up on the lonely earth-heart;
Doomed to be buried in the sea and chewed by fishes and worms,
Alas! It would be better to be used as firewood to burn that ice-cold life.
[October 1, 1926]

序曲

我也知道了,天地間什麼都有個結束;
最後,樹葉的欠伸也破了林中的寂寞。
原是和死一同睡著的,但這須臾的醒,
莫非是色的誘惑,聲的慫恿,動的罪惡?

這些摧殘的命運,汙濁的墮落的靈魂,
像是遺棄的屍骸亂鋪在淒涼的地心;
將來溺沉在海洋裏給魚蟲去咀嚼吧,
啊,不如當柴炭去燒燃那冰冷的人生。
十五,十,一。

PART ONE: HEAVEN AND MAY

1. Heaven

Chapter 1

Alas, this barren heaven--
Why is it no different from a beautiful tomb?
Lord on high!
You have lured everyone here to keep in captivity,
    Shutting out all human desires: 5
    Lord on high!

Coming here to heaven
Everything must be dedicated to you alone;
Everyone is devoted to being your slave.
If think, they think of you solely,   10
If they love, they love you only,
If unwilling, they pretend to be willing!
Lord on high!

You may also have a group of immortal maidens--
Actresses of the Lunar Palace,   15
Knocking on stone chimes coldly;
Playing bamboo flutes resentfully;
Singing songs inaudible to human ears;
Chanting unmoving poems.
But alas, everyone's ears hear merely breath--   20
And you are no different!
Lord on high!

You should know,
Love and selfishness are coalescing things,

Just like a model man cannot completely separate himself   25
From his impure thoughts;
But love's selfishness and selfishness's love
Are two different things, I'm afraid.
Lord on high!

Perhaps you yourself also truly believe   30
That heaven is full of joy
While this world is full of grief?

Yet this world's grief,
Is grief having solace;
Heavenly joy   35
Is only giving long-lasting athanasia to the long-lived,
Who partake of longevity pills.
Lord on high!

Lord on high!
I dare not accept your love!   40
Your love truly is a fire that,
In order to love water,
Burns all water dry.
Water falls in love with fire,
And they die together.   45
I dare not accept your love!
Lord on high!

Chapter 2

The apple trees in the green grass
Begin to blossom.

PART ONE: HEAVEN AND MAY

Lord on high! 50
You love it!
You whisper in a breath of wind;
Your tears of joy like light dewdrops.
The flowers smile; 55
Like a virgin falling in love with her first lover,
So they love you;
Apple trees have been blooming,
Which highlights your power!
Lord on high! 60

The apple trees have been blooming,
Getting bigger,
Getting plumper,
And finally mature;
You smile, 65
Smile with a watery mouth,
With thunder and raining
The fruit falls down.
It is your achievement.
Lord on high! 70

The fruit falls down,
He is the fruit of freedom,
Without any fetters;
He is the fruit of contentment,
He drops down anywhere 75
Feeling at ease wherever he has landed,
He does not beg to grow feet,
Nor if he had any

Would he run up to your heaven!
Alas, he is the fruit that you have produced! 80
Lord on high!

He is the fruit that you have produced.
You give him up and
Let him rot.
He leaves his root afterwards; 85
The root sprouts,
The sprout turns into a tree again,
The tree blossoms;
You fall in love with the tree again,
The blossoms bear fruit yet again; 90
You make use of your one-time-victory as a means
To achieve hundreds of victories with the same weaponry;
Surprisingly, you win!
You now own a garden of apple trees!
Lord on high! 95

In the garden of apple trees,
Full of apples--
Fruits of freedom,
Fruits of contentment,
Fruits of freedom and contentment, 100
Fruits of contentment and freedom,
Fruits of contentment and contentment,
Fruits of freedom and freedom.
Does all the fruit in the garden
Really belong to you? 105
Lord on high!

All the fruit in the garden,
You lock inside the garden's gate.
You forbid anyone else to hold anything back,
If other people have something themselves,   110
But yet you take it by force,
Locking it in the garden.
Does all the fruit in the garden
Really belong to you?
Lord on high!   115

Chapter 3

In front of the garden of apple trees
Sits a gatekeeper, Satan.
He can walk along the wall like a snake;
He can run wildly in the hills like a horse;
He can swim in the water like a fish,   120
He can soar in the sky like a bird;
Cunning is his nature,
And he is a master of seduction.
He just treats you as his only master.
Lord on high!   125

In front of the garden of apple trees
Lies a huge block of unfeeling stone.
On its edge
Lie two pitiful people.
Though they are different in gender,   130
Both of them know nothing about their sexual instincts.
They just sleep together;
Walk together;

Live together,
Live inside this, your heaven.   135
Lord on high!

Both of them know nothing about joy,
So they never feel joyful;
Both of them know nothing about grief,
So they never feel griefstricken;   140
Both of them know nothing about shame,
So they never feel shameful;
Both of them know nothing about anything,
So they can do nothing.
Oh, Lord on high!   145
Since you make them know nothing,
So that they are nothing,
Why did you allow them to be born?
Lord on high!

That day is the same day   150
Of your celebration.
The air bears the fragrance of apples,
Naturally arousing Satan's interest,
So he watches these two people:
Adam and   155
Eve,
Sitting together.
Satan is pondering the fruits in this garden,
And gives them some to show them how it tastes.
Oh, what a delicious thing to eat!   160
They think that everyone should have a taste!

PART ONE: HEAVEN AND MAY

Lord on high!

He ever so lightly unlocks the garden gate,
Stealthily concealing himself in the shade of a tree;
Singing a delightful song,   165
Chanting a seductive poem.
Adam hears.
Eve hears.
"Ah, I feel burning here."
Adam points to his face.   170
"Ah, I feel pounding here."
Eve points to her heart.
This is Satan's doing!
Lord on high!

Both of them are lured by the song and the poem,   175
Into the garden gate.
Ah, for both of them who have never tasted fruit,
The color of the fruit makes their mouths water;
Both of them are yearning to have a taste!
They feed some to each other!   180
All of sudden, they have knowledge!
But before they know all about
Joy, grief and shame,
First they know love!
Lord on high!   185
[April 16, 1926, Paris]

天堂

第一章

啊這枯燥的天堂,
何異美麗的墳墓?
上帝!
你將一切引誘來囚在裏面,
複將一切的需要關在外邊:
上帝!

來在這裏,
一切的一切便須貢獻給你;
犧牲了一切來做你的奴隸。
要想須想你,
要愛須愛你,
不願意也要願意!
上帝!

你雖然也有一班仙女——
月宮的戲子,
敲著冰冰冷的石磬;
吐著幽幽暗的鐵簫;
唱著不入耳的歌;
吟著不動心的詩。
呵只是一切的耳朵
和你自己的不同嚇!
上帝!

你要知道

PART ONE: HEAVEN AND MAY

愛和自私是連著的東西，
像好人難能完全脫離
壞的思想一般；
不過愛的自私與自私的愛
是兩樣東西嚇。
上帝！

你自己或許也真以為
天堂是快樂的吧；
人世是悲苦的吧？

但是人世的悲苦，
是有安慰的悲苦；
天堂的快樂，
只是給不死時的活人
吃的長生丹嚇。
上帝！

上帝！
我不敢領受你的愛嚇！
你的愛真是個火
為了愛水，
便把水燒幹了。
水被火愛了，
結果是個死。
我不敢領受你的愛嚇！
上帝！

第二章

青草叢裏的蘋果樹
開了花了。
上帝！
你愛了！
你吐著絮語的和風；
你流著清淚的輕露。
花笑了；
像處女愛第一個情人
一般地愛你了，
結果了，
是你的能力嚇！
上帝！

花結果了，
大了，
膨脹了，
圓滿了，
你笑了；
笑得瀎唾噴了，
雷嚇雨嚇，
果子落下來了。
是你的功勞嚇！
上帝！

果子落下來了，
是自由的果子嚇，
他沒有一切的束縛；
是知足的果子嚇，
他落下在那裏，
便安心在那裏，

PART ONE: HEAVEN AND MAY

他不求生腳,
更不求生了腳,
跑上你的天堂!
這是你造成的果子嚇!
上帝!

是你造成的果子嚇,
你棄著不理。
他腐爛了,
他留下了根而化了,
根發芽了,
芽又成樹了,
樹又開花了,
你又愛了,
花又結果了;
你以一次得勝的工具,
當百次得勝的兵器,
居然你得勝了!
有了個蘋果園。
上帝!

蘋果園中,
滿結著蘋果——
自由的果子,
知足的果子,
自由的知足的果子,
知足的自由的果子,
知足的知足的果子,
自由的自由的果子。
這滿園的果子嚇,

是你的？
上帝！

滿園的果子，
你又將園門鎖了。
你不准人家去取；
人家自己有的，
你也去奪了來，
關在園裏。
這滿園的果子嚇，
是你的？
上帝！

第三章

蘋果園前，
坐著個殺旦看門。
他會像蛇般在牆上行走；
他會像馬般在山中狂奔；
他會像魚般在水心游泳；
他會像鳥般在天空飛騰；
刁詐是他的性格，
誘引是他的技能。
他只以你當他的主人，
上帝！

蘋果園前，
有塊無知覺的大石，
大石邊上，
躺著兩個可憐的人們。

PART ONE: HEAVEN AND MAY

他倆雖然有性的分別,
只是誰也不知道
男女的本能。
他倆一起地睡著;
一起地走著;
一起地活著,
活在你這天堂裏面。
上帝!

他倆不知道快樂,
於是也不會快樂;
他倆不知道悲苦,
於是也不會悲苦;
他倆不知道羞恥,
於是也不會羞恥;
他倆不知道一切,
於是也不會一切!
上帝嚇!
你既然使他倆不知道一切,
而不一切,
那麼為甚要將他倆生了?
上帝!

恰好那一天,
又是你尋歡的日期。
空氣帶出了蘋果的香味,
自然提高了殺旦的興趣,
他看著他倆,
亞當,
夏娃,

坐在一起，
他想著這園中的果子，
也得使他倆嘗些滋味。
啊好吃的東西，
應得使人人嘗些滋味嚇！
上帝！

他輕輕地開了園門，
偷偷地藏入樹陰；
唱著入耳的歌，
吟著動心的詩。
亞當聽得了。
夏娃聽得了。
"啊我此地在燒。"
亞當指著臉。
"啊我此地在跳。"
夏娃指著心。
這是殺旦的工作了！
上帝！

他倆尋著歌詩，
進了園門。
啊沒吃到果子的人，
果子的顏色已使他們生津。
他倆嘗著試著！
相相地嘗試著！
他倆知道了！
但是他倆在知道
快樂悲苦羞恥一切從前，
先知道了愛！

PART ONE: HEAVEN AND MAY

上帝!
　　十五，四，十六，巴黎。

2. Sister Hua Mulan

Younger sister,
You should not forget your elder sister Hua Mulan.
She has worn
Armor as strong as that which dressed Yue Fei[1];
She has ridden a battle steed   5
As fast as that ridden by Guan Yu[2];
Like all other soldiers,
She has killed men in battle.

During such a black night
Every family cries out as   10
Family members depart to exchange
Their lives with the enemy's like pawns--
Their fathers, older brothers, younger brothers,
Husbands,
Younger uncles, older uncles, brother's sons, sister's sons, 15
Everyone's sons;
Your own son,
Your only son,
Two branches of a family combining into one son's son,
Sister Hua Mulan is also waiting for the best time   20

---

[1] Yue Fei (1103-1142) was a Han Chinese general who lived during the Southern Song dynasty, and was widely seen as a patriot and national folk hero. Since after his death, Yue Fei has evolved into a standard epitome of loyalty in Chinese culture.

[2] Guan Yu (died 220), courtesy name Yunchang, was a general serving under the warlord Liu Bei in the late Eastern Han dynasty. He played a significant role in the civil war that led to the collapse of the dynasty and the establishment of the state of Shu Han – founded by Liu Bei – in the Three Kingdoms period.

PART ONE: HEAVEN AND MAY

To exchange her flesh and blood!

Clip-clop, clip-clop,
Hoofbeats from a General's horse,
The marching tread of foot soldiers,
—And the sound of snickering from the God of Death: 25
"Ha-ha! Tonight or tomorrow night,
Living men created by God
From ten-month pregnancies,
And with many years' education
Will come before my roll sheet 30
To find their year, month, day and hour.
Ha-ha, why do you struggle to live?
You are surely born in order to die!

"Ha-ha! Look at them—my livestock!
As fat as cows, 35
As stupid as pigs,
As cowardly as sheep,
As shrill as roosters,
As stubborn as ducks,
As free as fish, 40
As lively as shrimp,
As … as ….
Ha-ha! Look at them—my livestock!
My morning meal,
My noon meal, 45
My midnight meal,
Ha-ha! Look at them—my livestock!
Some flesh and blood

Are just made ready for me to wine and dine."

The moon keeps its eyes open-- 50
It has gotten used to seeing all this!
Swords and spears shining,
Mirroring one image after another:
Some brightly reflect just a hand,
Some brightly reflect just a foot, 55
Some brightly reflect half a leg,
Some brightly reflect half the side of a shoulder,
Some brightly reflect a head,
Some ....
They are the mirrors of the warriors' fates, 60
Which they are grasping,
Dragging,
Carrying on their shoulders,
Bearing on their backs; 65
Gradually, the time comes near to discover them.

Sister Hua Mulan becomes even more beautiful
She applies more white powder than before,
She spreads on more red rouge,
She observes many, many foot soldiers-- 70
Many, many men--
They look like a herd of animals heading off for the slaughterhouse.
Some know they must die and resign themselves to it,
With a streaming flow of tears,
Others mistakenly believe they might survive and pretend to be gallant, 75

With sweat continually dripping,
You look at me and I look at you,
Wanting to speak the unspeakable,
Some like tigers,
Some like mice,   80
They are all by boredom compelled to cry out,
By terror forced to scream,
Frightened to die and yet equally unwilling to live,
Wanting to live yet equally willing to die.
She calls to mind her father,   85
She thinks of her aging father,
She thinks of her aging father,
Not having a strong young son,
She thinks of how it is thus convenient,
To temporarily hide her sweet little daughter's name,   90
Having recourse to a big man's heroic title,
Accepting the command to kill or to be killed,
Playing the dubious role to kill and to be killed.
She wears the helmet and armor of filial piety,
She rides the war horse of loyalty,   95
Bears under her arm the lance of righteousness,
Oh! She is altogether prepared for action!

The God of Death spreads out his wings,
And flies to and fro,
His two great wings   100
Just like two black curtains;
If something is veiled by them,
It will be veiled eternally,
Becoming a secret of secrets,

Making people invent absurd conjectures, 105
And concoct numerous unfounded facts,
To answer these unanswered questions;
The God of Death makes no affirmations,
Nor does he deny anything,
He just gradually produces one deception after another, 110
Making each one a mystery forever;
He flies into the Marshal's mind,
While he is ambitiously planning:
Imagining the flag of victory,
Planning to win the flag of victory, 115
Planning to conquer a magnificent city,
Planning to gain a massive reward,
Planning to achieve glorious fame.

The God of Death flies into the mind of a foot soldier,
Who is gloomily pondering: 120
Pondering beheading close kin,
Pondering a spear kissing his own heart,
Pondering the past which he cannot bear to remember,
Pondering the future which he dare not face.

The God of Death flies into the heart of the imperial palace, 125
And sees the emperor frolicking with the empress;
He flies to the edge of a field
And sees the peasant woman sobbing with her daughter-in-law.

The God of Death flies up to paradise,
Where Buddha tightly closes his eyes, 130

PART ONE: HEAVEN AND MAY

For Buddha is basically a pitiless being.
He flies down to the underworld,
Where Yaksha[1] stretches his neck
Waiting for new business to come.

The God of Death flies to Sister Hua Mulan's side,   135
Where he is greatly shocked and scared!
He senses no furious air,
Only ripples of soft perfume;
The light of chastity that she emits
Is too bright for him to open his eyes.   140

"A heart with no greed for fame,
Eyes with no lust for wealth,
And a mind with no impure thoughts,
How did such a person as this
Come to assemble here?   145
Alas, actually this slim waist
Is yet bounded by the net of circumstances;
Alas, how this poor slim waist
Is yet bounded by the net of circumstances."
As the God of Death thus reflects,   150
Remorse crowds into
His heart of stone.

The Moon suddenly clasps shut its eyes,

---

[1] Yaksha: In Hindu, Jain, and Buddhist texts, the yakṣa has a dual personality. On the one hand, a yakṣa may be an inoffensive nature-fairy, associated with woods and mountains; but there is also a darker version of the yakṣa, which is a kind of ghost (bhuta) that haunts the wilderness and waylays and devours travelers.

Anxious drums beat on all sides,
Gunfire cracks and flames 155
Flying aimlessly in the air,
And some of the soul's spirit has departed,
While some of the mind's vigor fades away.
Millions upon millions of bodies without soul or mind left:
Chopped down--falling, 160
Split open—being cut up,
Stabbed—being torn apart,
Flesh blown everywhere like a whirlwind
Blood reddens the ground like a rainstorm.

"Ah-ha-ha! 165
Living men's blood,
Dead men's flesh,
Dead men's blood,
Living men's flesh,
Ah-ha-ha!" 170
The laughter of the God of Death,
Shakes the earth and the sky:
"Kill, kill, kill!
You kill him,
I kill you, 175
He kills me,
He kills him,
Kill, kill, kill!
Kill, kill, kill!
I kill him, 180
He kills you,
You kill me,

PART ONE: HEAVEN AND MAY

He kills him,
Kill, kill, kill!

"Kill, kill, kill!   185
One kills one,
One kills two,
Two kill one,
Two kill two,
Kill, kill, kill!   90

"Die, die, die!
You die,
He dies,
I die,
Die, die, die!   195

"Die, die, die!
You half die,
He half dies,
I half die,
Die, die, die!   200

"Die, die, die!
You die, too,
He dies, too,
I die, too,
Die, die, die!   205

"Die, die, die!
One dies,

Two die,
Five die,
Ten die,   210
Die, die, die!

"Die, die, die!
Fifty die,
One hundred die,
One thousand die,   215
Ten thousand die,
Die, die, die!"

"Die, die, die!
Tens of thousands die,
Untold numbers die,   220
Die, die, die!"

"Ah-ha, kill, kill, kill!
Ah-ha, die, die, die!
Ah-ha, death endlessly kills!
Ah-ha, slaughter endlessly dies!"   225

Oh, the God of Death is so busy,
Oh, the God of Death is so busy,
Front,
Back,
Left,   230
Right,
Coming,
Going,

Oh, the God of Death is so busy!
Oh, the God of Death is so busy!   235

Oh, the God of Death is so busy!
Oh, the God of Death is so busy!
Aha!
Eating,
Drinking,   240
Drinking,
Eating,
Eating here,
Drinking there,
Eating over here,   245
Drinking over there,
Aha!
Oh, the God of death is so busy!
Oh, the God of death is so busy!

What is that sound?   250
Thunder--thunder dare not make a sound,
What is that sight?
Lightning--lightning dare not show up,
There is only--
Only--   255
Sword hitting spear,
Spear striking sword,
Sword knocking sword,
Spear against spear,
To live or to die,   260
To die or to live!

At daybreak,
The barbarians flee,
The government troops have won,
Sister Hua leads them,   265
The remnant of the living,
Foot soldiers,
Returning to their camp;
Ah, the death is done,
And living awaits!   270

The Moon hangs in the center of the sky,
Soldiers think it is only
The guiding light to the God of Death,
The biggest particle of phantom phosphorus.
But no,   275
Tonight it comes joyfully,
Congratulating them on their triumph,
On their slaying so many living men,
They are capable--and lucky.

Rewarding his soldiers according to merit,   280
The beaming Marshal
Thanks the generals and the soldiers,
Having prepared a variety of dishes,
And opened several jars of wine;
Everyone eats and drinks.   285
There is talking and chatting,
Shouting and singing,
By a casual estimate
It was all the price of flesh and blood,

The consolation of life!   290

Sister Hua inclines to her wine cup,
Very secretly wishing
Her father's good health,
And that all in the midst of danger
Might obtain peace.   295
Sister Hua, by this time
Has seen the affairs of this world,
And she knows that people are essentially not
Completely cruel;
Their cruelty, however, has been caused by unbroken prejudice,
      abetting   300
Its safe leap into the environment that lures it,
Forcing the living to
Pay a visit to the God of Death;
He calls you people to him,
Awakening all who are asleep   305
And keeping the sleeping from awakening.

She also knows
People's inclination to fight
Is not inborn;
Because they fear themselves dying,   310
Therefore they hate others living,
Raising their swords to resist spears,
Pulling out their swords to meet all blades;
But they are simply unaware
When blaming everyone else for wanting to take up the terrible
      tools,   315

That they should first give up their sharp weapons.

"Ah, people are selfish, selfish,"
She just puzzles,
"Perhaps that is their sin,
And thus the Creator sends them myriad torments;   320
Nevertheless, since the Creator is almighty,
He can create them as well as destroy them,
But why does he create them?"

Heaven's secrets must not be divulged,[1]
The mysteries of Buddha's dharma are impossible to make
    clear,   325
The Creator is so crafty and vicious,
That people cannot solve them and only store them
In their hearts.

In the sky there is a moon,
With scattered stars all around,   330
Sister Hua gazes at it all sadly;
She seems to understand,
But she does not--
It is the wailing nightingale who understands creation!
[November 6, 1925, Cambridge]

---

[1] Shao here uses the Chinese saying "*Tian ji bu ke xie lou.*"

PART ONE: HEAVEN AND MAY

花姊姊

妹妹,
不要忘了花姊姊
她也穿過了
嶽飛穿過了般的兵甲;
她也騎過了
關公騎過了般的戰馬;
跟了一般人
殺人。

似這般的黑夜,
家家哭著
和敵軍去交易生命的小卒。——
他們的爸爸,哥哥,弟弟,
丈夫,
叔叔,伯伯,侄子,甥兒,
兒子:
親生的兒子,
獨養兒子,
兩房合一子的兒子。
花姊姊,也便等著
匯兌血肉!

滴滴,苔苔,
大將的馬蹄聲,
小卒的足履聲,
——死神的竊笑聲:
"哈哈,今晚或是明朝,
上帝創造著的生靈

十月的懷胎,
多年的教養;
又當來在我的點名簿上
找他們的年月日時了。
哈哈,活著作甚?
本來是為了死而生的!

"哈哈他們,——我的畜牲!
像牛般肥胖的,
像豬般愚憨的,
像羊般懦怯的,
像雞般尖利的,
像鴨般頑固的,
像魚般瀟灑的,
像蝦般活潑的,
像⋯⋯⋯⋯⋯。
哈哈他們,——我的畜牲!
我的早餐,
我的午膳,
我的夜飯,
哈哈他們,——我的畜牲!
有的血肉,
本來是給我吃吃喝喝的。"

月兒仍張著眼,——
它看慣了的!
刀槍耀著,
早印著一個個影子:
有的照進去了只手,
有的照進去了只腳,

PART ONE: HEAVEN AND MAY

有的照進去了半條腿,
有的照進去了半壁肩,
有的照進去了個頭,
有的………。
這是他們運命的鏡子,
他們持著,
拖著,
扛著,
背著,
漸漸地近用著的時候了。

花姊姊更美麗了
她比往昔敷著粉更白,
她比往昔塗著脂更紅,
她看著多少的小卒——
多少的男兒——
好像一群進宰場的畜牲。
也有知道一定死而示弱的,
淚涔涔流的,
也有以為未必死而裝威的,
汗源源淌的,
你看看我我看看你的,
想說話說不出的,
有像虎的,
有像鼠的,
被煩悶逼著喊的,
被恐怖迫著叫的,
怕死而似乎不要活的,
想活而似乎情願死的。
她想到她的爸爸,

她想到她的老了的爸爸,
她想到她的老了的爸爸
沒有年壯的兒子;
她想到她如此便
暫藏了小女子的嬌名,
假借了大丈夫的英號,
受了殺人或是被人殺的命令,
來幹殺人或是被人殺的勾當。
她穿了孝的兵甲,
她騎了忠的戰馬,
她挾了義的長槍,
啊,她一切都預備好了!

死神展開了他的翅翼了,
飛來又飛去,
他的兩柄翅翼嚇
正像是兩張黑幕;
被他蒙蔽了的,
便永久蒙蔽著,
成了秘密的秘密;
使人們興起了不少荒謬的解釋,
使人們捏造了許多虛妄的事實,
來回答這沒回答的問題,
死神也不來辨明,
也不來否認,
只慢慢地將一個個來蒙蔽,
使一個個永久不明不白。
他飛到元帥的腦際,
元帥正雄雄勃勃地想著:
想著勝利的旗子,

PART ONE: HEAVEN AND MAY

想著偉大的城市,
想著厚重的酬賞,
想著光榮的名譽。

他飛到小卒的心頭,
小卒正幽幽鬱鬱地想著:
想著刀親人家的頭,
想著槍吻自己的心,
想著不忍想的過去,
想著不敢想的將來。

他飛到宮中,
皇帝對著後妃嬉笑;
他飛到田邊,
鄉婦同著女媳唏噓。

他飛到天上,
菩薩閉緊了眼,
菩薩本是無情的東西。
他飛到地下,
夜叉伸長了頸,
在等著這一筆的生意。

死神又飛到花姊姊的身旁,
他大大地詫異驚慌!
聞不到一些的殺氣,
只是陣陣的柔香;
貞潔之光
射得他的眼睛不能開張。

"心中沒有貪名的理想，
目中沒有求利的希望，
腦海中也沒有垢汙的波浪。
像這般的人
怎麼也會來到這個地方？
啊，原來這細細的腰兒，
也纏繞著環境的網。
啊，怎的這細細的腰兒，
也纏繞著環境的網；
啊，可憐著細細的腰兒
竟纏繞著環境的網。"
死神這般地思忖，
痛惜也擁進了他的
鐵石的心腸。

月兒忽然把眼睛一閉，
急鼓四起，
號炮聲中的火光
在空中亂飛，
有魂的魂走了，
有魄的魄遁去。
千千萬萬沒魂魄的肢體：
斬著——倒著，
劈著——斷著，
刺著——破著，
狂風般的肉花了天，
暴雨般的血染了地。

"啊啊，哈哈，
活人的血，

PART ONE: HEAVEN AND MAY

死人的肉,
死人的血,
活人的肉,
啊啊,哈哈!"
死神的笑嚇,
震動了天地:
殺殺殺!
你殺他,
我殺你,
他殺我,
他殺他,
殺殺殺!
殺殺殺!
我殺他,
他殺你,
你殺我,
他殺他,
殺殺殺!

殺殺殺!
一個殺一個,
一個殺兩個,
兩個殺一個,
兩個殺兩個,
殺殺殺!

死死死!
你死,
他死,
我死,

THE VERSE OF SHAO XUNMEI

死死死！

死死死！
你半死，
他半死，
我半死，
死死死！

死死死！
你也死，
他也死，
我也死，
死死死！

死死死！
一個死
兩個死，
五個死，
十個死，
死死死！

死死死！
五十個死，
一百個死，
一千個死，
一萬個死，
死死死！

死死死！
幾萬個死，

PART ONE: HEAVEN AND MAY

多多少少個死,
死死死!

啊啊, 殺殺殺!
啊啊, 死死死!
啊啊, 死不盡的殺!
啊啊, 殺不盡的死!

啊啊死神真忙嚇,
啊啊死神真忙嚇,
前嚇,
後嚇,
左嚇,
右嚇,
來嚇,
去嚇,
啊啊死神真忙嚇!
啊啊死神真忙嚇!

啊啊死神真忙啊!
啊啊死神真忙啊!
啊啊,
吃嚇,
喝嚇,
喝嚇,
吃嚇,
這裏吃嚇,
那邊喝嚇,
這邊吃嚇,
那裏喝嚇,

啊啊！
啊啊死神真忙嚇！
啊啊死神真忙嚇！

什麼？
雷——雷不敢作聲，
什麼？
電——電不敢現形，
只是——
只是——
刀碰槍，
槍觸刀，
刀打刀，
槍對槍，
生生死死，
死死生生！

天明了，
番將逃了，
官兵勝了，
花姊姊領著，
死剩的活的，
小卒，
回營交令；
啊，死的完了
活的等著！

月兒又掛上天心，
小卒只以為是
引見死神的導燈，

PART ONE: HEAVEN AND MAY

最大的一粒鬼磷。
啊不,
今夜它是來道喜的,
賀你們的得勝,
殺死了多少的活人,
能幹——僥倖。

論功行賞,
元帥笑嘻嘻地
謝著大將小卒,
備了幾樣菜,
開了幾氅酒;
大家吃喝。
說說談談,
叫叫唱唱,
只便算是
血肉的代價,
生命的安慰了!

花姊姊也傾了一盞,
暗暗地祝著
爸爸康健,
大家在危險中
都得到安寧。
花姊姊,這一次嚇
見到了不少事情,
她知道人們本不是
絕對的殘忍,
那只是受了
打不破的見解的慫恿,

跳不出的環境的誘引，
逼著活人
拜見死神；
叫你們人
醒的都睡，
睡的不醒。

她又知道
人們的爭鬥性，
也不是天生，
為了怕自己死，
所以恨別人生；
提刀為的是抵槍，
拔劍為的是遇刃；
但他們只沒知道
怪人家要拿起兇器，
應當自己先棄去了利兵。

"啊，自私自私，"
她只是疑惑著，
"也許這便是人們的罪名，
因而造物給以種種的苦刑；
不過造物萬靈
既生之而複滅之，
為什麼不使之不生？"

天機的秘密不可洩露，
佛法的玄妙萬難道明，
造物的狡獪（惡毒）
只能也不解而存在

PART ONE: HEAVEN AND MAY

凡人的中心。

中天一個月亮,
四面散著疏星,
花姊姊悶悶的凝望;
她像懂得,
她沒懂得,
懂的是那
哀叫的一隻夜鶯。
　十四,十一,六,劍橋。

3. Hair

Ah, hair of Mélisande[1],
Under the moonlight you are part of the moon's brightness,
Coiling around the neck of your lover one hair after another.

Ah, Lady Fermor's hair, [2]
By a merciless hand a lock has been cut,   5
And turns out to be written into a masterpiece by a merciful hand.

Ah, on this cheek so white like the snow-capped North Pole,
Comes floating a wave of peony pink;
Those eyes and their brow tips and her hair bun,
Just like an otter resting beside a shore.   10

A breeze blows loose her hair bun,
Which falls down in disarray upon her shoulders.
The Jade Rabbit in the Moon Palace saw it from afar,
Doubting the Moon Goddess has again left her paradise.

Awaking from a midnight dream,   15
Black cloud upon the white pillow:
Making appear this contrasting red star,
Like a celestial hound I wildly gulp it down.

---

[1] See Achille-Claude Debussy and his opera "Pelléas et Mélesandè" in 1902.
[2] Arabella Fermor was Alexander Pope's friend whose lock had been cut by Lord Peter. This incident has been written into Pope's poem *The Rape of the Lock* in 1712.

Ah, the hair of a lover,
Weaving a knot in the bottom of her lover's heart;   20
In such a short and fast time, every minute and every second,
The lover is busy with disentangling this endless hair-knot.
[January 31, 1926, Cambridge]

頭髮

梅李霜特的頭髮嚇,
你在明月下與明月爭光,
又一根根繞在你情人的頸上。

法摩夫人的頭髮嚇,
被無情的手剪去了一束,
竟使有情的手寫成了不朽之作。

啊這北極雪般白的頰上,
漂來一層淡紅芍藥色的輕浪;
那眼球眉梢及髮鬢,
又像水獺休息在岸旁。

和風吹松了髮髻,
髮髻散披在肩上。
玉兔在月宮中望見了,
疑是嫦娥又離了天堂。

後半夜的夢醒,
白枕上的烏雲:
襯托出這一點紅星,
我將像天狗般狂吞。

啊情人的頭髮嚇,
在情人心中打著結;
情人在這最短最快的時光裏嚇,
分分秒秒只是去解這無窮的結吧。
　　　　十五, 一, 三一, 劍橋。

4. Narcissus

Ah, Narcissus!
Since you grow inside this filthy mire,
Why you still possess this certain perfume that
Attracts passerby like me to love you?

Ah, Narcissus! 5
I step into the mud to kiss you with my mouth,
But how can I pick you up?
You are long since sunk in this filthy mire!

Wind comes and wind kisses you,
Rain comes and rain kisses you. 10
Why not you escape or hide yourself,
Instead of standing smilingly erect in the filthy mire!

Have you lost your senses?
Then how can you have any affection for me?
Alas! Isn't it better to speak a little with you about love, then? 15
Better let you alone and dwell in the filthy mire!
[January 21, 1926, Cambridge]

水仙嚇

水仙嚇！
你既然生在這汙濁的泥裏，
為什麼還要有這一些的香氣，
竟使過路的我也想愛你？

水仙嚇！
我踏進了泥裏把嘴來吻你，
但我又怎能將你采起？
你早已落在這汙濁的泥裏！

風來風吻你，
雨來雨吻你。
你為什麼不逃遁或是躲避，
還笑盈盈地立在這汙濁的泥裏？

你是不是已失卻了知覺，
那麼對我猶怎會有情意？
啊和你來講些什麼愛呢？
還是讓你住在這汙濁的泥裏！
　　　十五，一，二一，劍橋。

5. A Poem

Tears run down her face in the form of a Y,
Her struggling breath and
Her fast-beating heart *harmonize* finally;
She puts her trouble into the back of her mind,
In her handkerchief twisted in her hands:
She is fallen asleep on her long pillow--
Ah, the same dream for the fifteen years!
[Feb. 25, 1926, London]

一首詩

淚水在她臉上寫著 Y，
掙紮的呼吸和
奔跑的心跳 harmonize 了；
她又將胸懷裏的煩惱，
寄託在手中打了結的帕上；
她又靠著長枕睡去了——
啊十五年一樣的夢！
十五，二，二五，倫敦。

PART ONE: HEAVEN AND MAY

6. I Have to Be a Contented Insect

Gold-shod sun,
White marble *Venus de Milo*;
You are both what I
Earnestly thirst for as my cup of Longjing tea[1] when it is time
  to love.

My life is just like the grass sprouting from the earth's surface,
                                                                5
Evil-inducing rain and dew once fed me with their seed;
At sweet times, evil is sweet,
I fled from the midst of hell and found myself in this den of
  monsters.

I knew that clouds have capricious colors;
I have experienced coming from all directions this roving wind;
                                                               10
What I have understood and yet again not understood,
Is the vast firmament accompanying it all.

Could you tell me,
Is this not then the master of desire?
He exploits me with His exhausting endless cycle of life and
  death,   15
And cheats us of our beauty, pure water and green hills.

---

[1] Longjing Tea is regarded as the best tea in China and is produced near the West Lake, Hangzhou, Zhejiang Province.

He boasted before of His omnipotence,
But I have never seen Him come down to Earth.
He has just four garments: one wet, one dry,
One bright, one dark.   20

He cannot come here--the *Louvre*,
And He cannot get into the *Moulin Rouge*.
Alas! The omnipotent God,
Has thus lost His two greatest honors.

Oh, prophets who would not find a solution and sages who
    could not find the way   25
Seem wrapped in a mysterious mist.
I am just like a contented insect who
For a bright future willingly throws himself into the middle of
    the spider's web.

Oh, gold-shod sun,
You must save me when I wander too far!   30
Oh, white marble *Venus de Milo*
You must lend me a hand when yours is already broken off!
[Au Musee du Louvre, March, 1926]

PART ONE: HEAVEN AND MAY

我只得也像一隻知足的小蟲

金鞋子的太陽,
白石的 Venus de Milo;
你們都是我
苦渴著愛時龍井的杯茶。

我生命像草芽已長出土面
誘惡的雨露曾餵我以精液;
甜蜜時罪惡是甜蜜的,
我竟從地獄中逃來這地獄的魔窟。

我知道了雲有善變的顏色;
見到了南北東西流蕩的浪漫之風;
我所明白的而又不明白的,
是陪伴著一切的高高太空。

你能對我說嗎,
這是否便是欲望的主宰?
他欺我以生之不盡死之無窮,
騙去了我們的美人白水青山。

他曾誇言他底萬能,
我卻從未見他來在地上。
他只有一件濕一件幹,
一件明一件暗的四件衣裳。

他來不到這裏——Louvre
也走不進 Moulin Rouge
啊萬能的上帝嚇,

已失掉了兩件莫大的榮譽。

啊先知所不肯解聖人所不能道的
像霧罩在霧裏的神秘嚇,
我只得也像一隻知足的小蟲
為趨迎著光明而投身入蛛網中吧。

啊金鞋子的太陽,
你要救我路又遠遙!
啊白石的 Venus de Milo
你要援我你手已斷了!
[Au Musee du Louvre, March 1926]

7. Complete Recovery

For some days I have not seen Paris,
Even the wind there seems old already.
If not, why has it become so rough
When it blows into my face?

Paris, my own Paris, 5
How many times have I ever forgotten you?
I saw you again in a dream last night--
I dreamt of you as a camellia girl.[1]

So lovely are you,
How could I wish for everyone to come and adore you? 10
But I am afraid of going to the country with you,
For there you will loathe facing me all the time.

Thinking like this makes me weary,
So step by small step I return.
All is all in the end, 15
All is eventually all in the end!
[April 1, 1926]

---

[1] Alexandre Dumas, fils (1824–1895) was a French writer and dramatist, and was best known for *Camille* (a.k.a. *The Lady of the Camellias*).

病痊

幾天不見巴黎,
巴黎的風也已老了。
否則怎麼竟會
吹到臉上粗糙不少?

巴黎我底巴黎,
我幾時曾忘卻了你?
我昨夜又夢見——
夢見你便是茶花女。

這樣可愛的你,
我怎願人人來戀顧?
但怕同去鄉間,
你要嫌只對著個我。

想想人又倦了,
一步分兩步地回去。
一切是一切底,
一切終久是一切底!
十五,四,一,謄正。

8. Sappho

The fragrance of lotus leaves spreads the color of green,
The rose of the sun paints on the paper of the sky;
May, like the charcoal fire in the oven of evil,
Hotly kisses the shoots of passion.

Where does Sappho go, the player of the seven-stringed lyre? 5
Could it be that it is not granted for her to meet Eros in her
    dreams?
Ah, even if thousands of miles away,
Do come back right away!

Come back riding in your golden phoenix carriage,
To sing an ode to your co-existence with the cosmos-- 10
As beautiful as a virgin bride on a wedding bed
Is this lovely ode.

You should sit on a stone boat covered in reeds and sing,
Putting the turbulent waves to sleep with your song;
Even those merciless stones might be touched, 15
Lost in thought as they listen.

Those girls with Lesbian love,
You too cannot escape from ceaseless May's burning grill!
The oven of evil is already as red as blood,
It is time for you to enter it. 20

Your constant wet tears do not burn away?
Rain falling on Earth can rise to the sky and turn into clouds.

Why no happiness in the oven of evil?
Only you understand.

It seems that there is a voice in the sky calling: 25
"Sappho, do you have any unutterable sufferings?
Speaking the unutterable is even more bitter than keeping si-
    lent,
Nevertheless, you had better just say it!"

Waves come flying to you like white seagulls,
One eddy after another throws its seductive eyes upon you. 30
You remain sitting there without a word?
Alas! My dear Sappho!
[April 14 [no year], Paris]

PART ONE: HEAVEN AND MAY

莎茀

蓮葉的香氣散著青的顏色,
太陽的玫瑰畫在天的紙上;
罪惡之爐的炭火的五月嚇,
熱吻著情苗。

彈七弦琴的莎茀那裏去了,
莫非不與愛神從夢中相見?
啊盡使是一千一萬裏遠嚇,
請立刻回來。

你坐在你底金鑾車而來吧,
來唱你和宇宙同存的頌歌——
像新婚床上處女一般美的,
愛的頌歌嚇。

你坐在蘆蓋艇石上而唱吧,
將洶湧的浪濤唱得都睡眠;
那無情的亂石也許有感呢,
聽得都發呆。

藍筒布的同性愛的女子嚇,
你也逃避不了五月的燒炙!
罪惡之爐已紅得血一般了,
你便進去吧。

你底常濕的眼淚燒不幹嗎?
下地的雨都能上天成雲呢。
罪惡之爐中豈沒有快樂在?

只須你懂得。

仿佛有個聲音在空中喚著:
"莎茀你有什麼說不出的苦?
說不出不說出當更加苦呢,
還是說了吧!"

海水像白鷗般地向你飛來,
一個個漩渦都對你做眉眼,
你仍坐著不響只是不響嗎?
咳我底莎茀!
　四,十四,巴黎。

PART ONE: HEAVEN AND MAY

9. The Third Day of Floating on the Sea

It is my third day of floating on the sea,
Waves have blanketed the water's smiling face.
Ah, how many secrets are buried in the depths of the depths?
Lo, it seems to be the breast of a complaining spinster,
Full of exhausting struggles and unspeakable worries.   5
Lo, it seems to be the eyes of a lover,
Filled with teardrops still waiting to be crushed one day.
In the midst of the moon-tinted sea I ponder alone--
On the corner of clouds lies the dark forest,
Or the peak of Olympus?   10
Are the sobs near my ears,
The sound of Apollo's harp?
Ah, the heartstrings of a homesick ashamed wanderer
Cannot be constantly stricken by derision!
[May 24, 1926, Mediterranean]

漂浮在海上的第三天

是我漂浮在海上的第三天,
浪濤覆蓋了水面底笑顏。
啊這不見的深深裏有幾許秘密?
看嚇好像是怨女底胸膛,
蘊藏著盡掙紮而猶不敢訴說的心事。
看嚇好像是情人底眼睛,
包含了淚珠還待破碎的一日。
月光海色中間的我獨自思索——
雲角上是否烏暗的森林,
Olympus 之山巔?
我耳邊嗚咽著的,
是否 Apollo 底琴聲?
啊歸家的遊子底慚愧的心弦,
更怎當得譏誚底連續的撥彈!
　十五,五,二四,地中海。

PART ONE: HEAVEN AND MAY

10. Troubled

You are accompanying the child bride near the cooking stove,
The blood-red firewood has turned ice cold;
Again you are producing spring rain-like teardrops,
Ceaselessly devoting them.

In the thicket at the bottom of first loves' hearts,   5
You also once held in your mouth the twigs and leaves
To build your nest of love;
Your open heart often turns dim and dark.

Ah, your cowardly brothers!
Ah, your terrified parents!   10
If you had also been as licentious as the peach flower,
I would have plucked you already!
[May 29 [no year], Red Sea]

憂愁

你伴著養媳在灶前,
血紅的柴火也冰冷了;
你複將春雨般的淚珠,
不停地貢獻。

初戀者底心叢中,
你也曾銜了枝枝葉葉
去造個窩窟;
光明的胸懷便時常幽黑。

啊你懦怯底兄弟!
啊你恐怖底父母!
你要是也像桃花般淫蕩,
我便也將你採摘!
　五,二九,紅海。

11. A Sonnet

Among rare leaves of the tree of life,
Twenty-one have been picked by the days and years.
Hiding himself in his nest among the branches is a little bird,
Yet with no chance to try out his God-given wings;
He once adjusted his tender voice to be guttural,   5
But there is a curtain of muddy mist so thick and hard,
Blocking people in it from hearing.
Alas! These frail and rare leaves,
How many twenty-ones among them if counted?
That is the most patient and greedy moment,   10
Always looting them with his brutal and ruthless hands.
Emaciated new branches are thus laid bare,
Rain tears have emotionally moved the heart of the bird,
Who wants to fly to the clouds and comfort heaven.
[May 30, 1926 Red Sea]

十四行詩

生命之樹底稀少的葉子,
被時光摘去二十一片了。
躲藏在枝間巢中的小鳥,
還沒試用他天賜的羽翼;
他曾低弄他細嫩的喉音,
但有汙濁而堅厚的霧幕,
擋住著幕中人不能聽得。
啊這柔嫩而稀少的葉子,
片片數來有幾個二十一?
那最忍耐而貪婪的時光,
總用他兇殘的手來採摘。
枯瘦的新枝根根暴露了,
雨淚打動了小鳥底心靈,
想去雲間慰安天底悲哀。
十五,五,三十,紅海。

12. Love

On the sea's surface millions of bright fish
Play in little waves together;
This is simply love.
This is love's essence.

A mountain falls asleep in the fog,   5
And fog holds it in its bosom;
This is simply love.
This is love's principle.

Little raindrops passionately kiss the sea,
And the sea swallows them down into her heart;   10
This is simply love.
This is love's mystery.

Seawater calls the moon and gets no answer,
Little waves turn into flowing teardrops;
This is simply love.   15
This is love's flavor.
[June 4, 1926, Indian Ocean]

愛

海面千萬條光魚
和浪兒拼在一起；
這便是愛，
這便是愛的真諦。

一条山睡在霧裏，
霧將山攏在懷裏；
這便是愛，
這便是愛的原理。

雨珠兒盡吻著海，
海將雨吞在心裏；
這便是愛，
這便是愛的神秘。

海水叫月月不語，
浪兒化作點點淚；
這便是愛，
這便是愛的滋味。
 十五，六，四，印度洋。

PART ONE: HEAVEN AND MAY

13. The Poet and Jesus

Into this world comes the poet,
The starved family has one more mouth to feed.
Ah, maiden parent's son of God, Jesus,
The poet unfortunately is not in your image,
The poet has but one mother and one father.   5

The poet has but one mother and one father.
Nobody believes that he bears on his shoulders a mission as weighty as yours!
Your mission is to lead the half believing into heaven,
Disbelief you drive into damnation;
The mission of the poet is to cry out to others to build a heaven for themselves,   10
And himself destroy this hell.

But yours is the clear instruction of the saints,
While his is the somniloquy of the idiots;
Yours can persuade myriad foolish listeners,
His can only be believed by himself,   15
And maybe other people who are as crazy as him.
Ah, the poet unfortunately has but one mother and one father.

You on the cross have surpassed all,
The poet still by himself drinks his own tears.
Your soul is immortal,   20
Ha-ha! The poet laughs at your deathlessness.
[undated]

詩人與耶穌

世界上來了個詩人,
沒飯吃的家裏多了個吃飯的。
啊處女的親兒天主的愛子耶穌嚇,
詩人可惜不像你嚇,
詩人可惜有了個娘又有個爹。

詩人可惜有了個娘又有個爹。
但誰也不認為他負有著比你更重的使命!
你的使命是將信你的迎上天堂,
不信你的趕下地獄;
詩人的使命是叫人家自己造個天堂,
自己毀這地獄。

但是你的是聖者的明示,
他的是癡人的夢囈;
你的能說服萬千的愚魯的聽眾,
他的只能取信於他自己,
或是和他一般的瘋子。
啊詩人可惜有了個娘又有個爹。

你在十字架上超升了,
詩人還在自己飲自己的眼淚。
你的靈魂永生,
哈哈詩人在笑你的不死。
　(未記日期)

14. A Little Candle

I

The bright moon says to me:
    "Xunmei!
  You go light a little candle
    To lighten up the places where I cannot."

II

The white cloud is gray in the night--
My lover!
Do you know me?

III

The white-headed bird lowers her head
And sees little cherries
  Become redder and redder day after day.

IV

After the lamp is extinguished--
The lover's love
  Says to a nameless force:
"It is your world now."

V

The white cloud--
  Comes gently bearing something dreamlike!
  And departs poetically leaving behind something deathlike!

VI

The Sun falls asleep,
The Moon wakes up.
Ah, the door to heaven and hell
Is always open forever.

VII

The green grass on the other side of the river says nothing.
Ah, the river water plays a melody.

VIII

May!
You will go away sooner or later....
[undated]

PART ONE: HEAVEN AND MAY

小燭

【一】

明月對我說：
"洵美！
你去點枝小燭
　在我照不到的地方。"

【二】

白雲在黑夜中是灰的——
愛人！
你認識我麼？

【三】

白頭鳥低下頭去了
他看見櫻桃
一天比一天紅了

【四】

熄燈以後——
情人的愛
和一個不知名的勢力說：
"現在是你的世界了。"

【五】

白雲——
像夢一般帶著文氣來了！
像死一般留著詩意去了！

【六】

太陽睡了，
月亮醒了。
啊天堂地獄的門
是永久開著的嚇。

【七】

隔岸的青草不說話。
啊，河水在彈琴。

【八】

五月！
你是早晚要去的……
　（未記日期）

May Poems
五月之什

15. Song of Love

Jasper-like Heavenly Pond,
White jade-like lotus:
The lotus lives only in Heavenly Pond,
And Heavenly Pond bears only lotus.

Heavenly Pond is simply you,   5
The lotus is simply me:
I live only in your heart,
And you live only with me in your heart.
[Nov. 27, 1925]

PART ONE: HEAVEN AND MAY

戀歌

碧玉的天池，
白璧的雲荷：
雲荷只生在天池中，
天池中只生著雲荷。

天池便是你，
雲荷便是我；
我只生在你的心中，
你心中只生著個我。
十四，十一，二七。

16. Tomorrow

These yellow flowers finally bloom,
Everything blooms,
On the way of the air,
Birds busily come and go.

Clear dewdrops are kissing the green grass,
Which giggles;
Kissing and hugging,
They merge into one.

The flowing spring's voice is lower and lower;
Crying upward in the dark night,
The red sun answers the call,
This is hope's reward.

Neither begrudges the early daybreak,
Awakening after so long;
Beholding the beautiful green sky,
And trying on that jade-like coat of white clouds.
[December 6, 1925, Cambridge]

PART ONE: HEAVEN AND MAY

明天

這朵黃花竟然開了,
一切都開了,
空氣的道上,
複忙著來往的行鳥。

白露兒盡吻著青草,
青草格格笑;
吻著又擁抱,
擁抱到相相混沌了。

流泉聲一聲聲低了;
黑夜中高叫,
叫來了紅日,
這便是希望的酬報。

他倆也不嫌天明早,
醒了好久了;
看美的綠天,
試穿那玉的白雲襖。
十四,十二,六,劍橋。

17. Love

Who has heard that love should be like this?
Who has ever seen that love should be like this?
Ah, where is love?
Where does love live?

The little stone, for a kiss from the running spring water,
Is waiting morning and night in the cold mountain ravine;
Love once was here,
Love often visits here.

Night comes here, and the sun must go somewhere,
The moon will grant some of her brightness;
Love is here, too,
Love is habitually here.

Spring, summer, autumn and winter come by turns,
Four seasons existing eternally in the universe;
Love is always here,
Love loves to be here.
[January 15, 1926, Cambridge]

PART ONE: HEAVEN AND MAY

愛

誰沒聽到愛是這樣這樣的？
誰曾見得愛是怎般怎般的？
啊愛在那裏，
愛住在那裏？

為了要和流泉接吻的小石，
早晚地在這冷山澗中候著；
愛曾在這裏，
愛常在這裏。

夜來了太陽便須走向別處，
月兒因將所有的光陰賜與；
愛也在這裏，
愛慣在這裏。

春了夏夏了秋秋了又是冬，
四季永久生存在宇宙之中；
愛總在這裏，
愛愛在這裏。
十五，一，十五，劍橋。

18. Horror

In the bottom of my heart remains a small photo of you,
From my mouth have vanished the traces of your lips;
Sunshine's red rays have already gathered on the shoulders of
    the mountain,
Ah, that time for lamp lighting must come.

In my nose still lingers your dirty perfume,   5
Before my eyes is always your bloody guilty skin;
Sunshine's red rays have already gathered on the shoulders of
    the mountain,
Ah, that time for lamp lighting must come.
[April 12, 1926, Paris]

PART ONE: HEAVEN AND MAY

恐怖

我底心中還留著你底小影,
我底嘴上卻消了你底唇痕;
太陽的紅光已聚在山肩了,
啊那上燈的時分又要到了。

鼻裏不絕你那齷齪的香氣,
眼前總有你那血般的罪肌;
太陽的紅光已聚在山肩了,
啊那上燈的時分又要到了。
　十五,四,十二,巴黎。

19. Spring

Ah, this flower's perfume now always smells fleshly,
The unspeaking drizzle also harbors lust;
Bathing I hate to see my own guilty skin,
Ah, how to scour off the crimson on my body?
[June 6, 1927 in Baixia]

PART ONE: HEAVEN AND MAY

春

啊這時的花香總帶著肉氣，
不說話的雨絲也含著淫意；
沐浴恨見自己的罪的肌膚，
啊身上的緋紅怎能擦掉去？
（一六，六，六白下）

20. Summer

The pure white moonlight lightly tones the deep blue sky,
Sultry and oppressed cries are barred up in the throat;
Ah, quickly offer some love talk as tender as your tongue,
Cramming into my mouth which feels suffocated.
[April 15, 1926, Paris]

PART ONE: HEAVEN AND MAY

夏

純白的月光調淡了深藍的天色，
熱悶的喊叫都硬關住在喉嚨裏；
啊快將你情話一般溫柔的舌兒
來塞滿了我這好像不透氣的嘴。
　十五，四，二六，巴黎。

21. Flower

Heaven and Earth wed and gave birth to him,
Educated by Nature, gradually he grew up;
He came to know what is love,
He came to know what is beauty.

He was filled with lyrical beauty, 5
Was soundless music's embodiment;
Even if he had nothing more to offer,
He had already achieved his duty in life.

He had no sisters and no brothers,
He was unaware of boredom; 10
The vast universe was his home,
Branches and leaves were his companions.

He loved looking down at the stream bed,
Flowing with laughter toward unobstructed land;
Sometimes small stones blocked it midway, 15
But the stream leapt over them lightly.

He also loved the white clouds above his head,
For their aloof and noble spirit;
Though sometimes his friends were discouraged,
Still they never lapsed. 20

He loved wind for its never being fettered,
Blowing itself carefree in all directions;
It had set foot on the highest mountaintops,

PART ONE: HEAVEN AND MAY

And kissed all over the seas and oceans.

He had known the instinct of the sun,   25
He had known the purity of the moon;
Instinct does not result from time,
And purity's way has white brilliance.

He most feared that sad songbird,
Making complaints in the sweet sky;   30
Clearly the joyful harmony,
Was refusing to suppress its wail.

He pitied that dirty stinking world,
And sympathized with people who lose out to the corrupt;
He hoped for the patient raindrops,   35
To wash off the greasy filth one by one.

He gulped down the liquor of divine spirits,
And exhaled his own perfumed breath;
Making of hell a bridge into heaven,
Destroying all worry and loss.   40
[June 1, 1926, Indian Ocean]

花

天和地結婚便生了他,
自然教育著漸漸長大;
他知道了什麼是愛,
他知道了什麼是美。

他充滿了詩詞的美麗,
是無聲的音樂的具體;
便沒別的貢獻添助,
也盡了生命的義務。

他沒有姊妹沒有兄弟,
他不覺無聊反覺有趣:
大宇宙是他底宅寓,
枝和葉是他底伴侶。

他愛看他足下的溪溝,
向著無障礙處笑著流;
有時小石攔住中途,
他便從他身上跳過。

他也愛他頭上的白雲,
有超脫和高尚的精神;
雖有時友朋著灰濁,
但幾曾有一次墮落。

他愛風不被環境束縛,
自由地逍遙東西南北;
曾踏盡高山底頂蓋,

PART ONE: HEAVEN AND MAY

也曾吻遍了洋與海。

他知道了太陽底本能,
他知道了月亮底潔淨;
本能不是時間造成,
潔淨方有白的光明。

他最怕那悲哀的鳴鳥,
在甜蜜的空中說牢騷;
明明是快樂的歌調,
卻含著眼淚來呼號。

他惜著那腥穢的世界,
憐著人們被齷齪淘汰;
他希望忍耐的雨珠,
把這汙漬一一洗去。

他便吞了仙神的露漿,
吐出了他氣息的芬芳;
將地獄染成了天堂,
一切煩惱消滅淪亡。
十五,六,一,印度洋。

22. May

Ah, passionate May is burning again,
Evil is born in a virgin's kiss;
Sweet tear juice is always seducing me
To put my trembling lips upon her cleavage.

Life here seems as endless as death,   5
As fearful as a bridegroom on the happy wedding night;
If she is not a white rose,
Then she must be redder than red blood.

Ah, fire-like and flesh-like,
Bright darkness and laughing sobs,   10
Are of my love's soul's soul;
They are my hate's enemy's enemy.

Heaven opens wide its two-leaf door,
Oh, God, I am not the person to enter.
I have already found solace in hell,   15
I once dreamt of being awake on short nights.
[June 10, 1926]

PART ONE: HEAVEN AND MAY

五月

啊欲情的五月又在燃燒,
罪惡在處女的吻中生了;
甜蜜的淚汁總引誘著我
將顫抖的唇親她的乳壕。

這裏的生命像死般無窮,
像是新婚晚快樂的惶恐;
要是她不是朵白的玫瑰,
那麼她將比紅的血更紅。

啊這火一般的肉一般的
光明的黑暗嬉笑的哭泣,
是我戀愛的靈魂的靈魂;
是我怨恨的仇敵的仇敵。

天堂正開好了兩扇大門,
上帝嚇我不是進去的人。
我在地獄裏已得到安慰,
我在短夜中曾夢著過醒。
十五,六,十。

23. To Sappho

You, the perfume awaking from the flowerbed,
Just like a virgin's moonlit nakedness--
I have not beheld your skin of fire and blood,
But you are like a red rose opening in my heart.
[June 20, 1926, China Sea]

PART ONE: HEAVEN AND MAY

致莎茀

你這從花床中醒來的香氣,
也像處女的明月般裸體——
我不見你包著火血的肌膚,
你卻像玫瑰般開在我心裏。
十五,六,二〇,中國海。

24. To Swinburne

You are Sappho's older brother and I am her younger brother,
Our parents are God, who is the creator of Venus—
Sunglow, rainbow, the colorful tail of a peacock, the feathers
    of a phoenix,
The creation of all beautiful things is their work.

You love her, I also love her and love you, too;   5
Both of us prefer love and the mystery of love;
Both of us prefer the pure union of blood and flesh;
Both of us prefer the poisonous nectar and the bittersweet.

Ah, we three are just like wildflowers on a barren mountain,
We three refuse to be cultivated in flowerpots and arranged in
    vases;   10
We three come from mud and result in mud,
Thus our hope is to stay in mud forever.
[June 20, 1926, China Sea]

PART ONE: HEAVEN AND MAY

致史文朋

你是莎茀的哥哥我是她的弟弟,
我們的父母是造維納絲的上帝——
霞嚇虹嚇孔雀的尾和鳳凰的羽,
一切美的誕生都是他倆的技藝。

你喜歡她我也喜歡她又喜歡你;
我們又都喜歡愛喜歡愛的神秘;
我們喜歡血和肉的純潔的結合;
我們喜歡毒的仙漿及苦的甜味。

啊我們像是荒山上的三朵野花,
我們不讓人種在盆裏插在瓶裏;
我們從瀾泥裏來仍向瀾泥裏去,
我們的希望便是永久在瀾泥裏。
十五,六,二十,中國海。

25. I Cannot Stand

I cannot stand, I cannot stand!
White frost cannot depart from the autumn night's black;
Above Earth is heaven day after day,
Ah, how could I not see her for a moment?

I cannot stand, I cannot stand!
A lamp looked at the moon and the moon at the lamp;
The lady of the breeze comes leisurely by chance,
I want to embrace her but feel pain in my heart.
[August 20, 1926, midnight]

PART ONE: HEAVEN AND MAY

我忍不住了

我忍不住了我忍不住了！
白露總離不了秋的黑夜；
地的上面天天有個天在，
啊我怎能有一忽不見她？

我忍不住了我忍不住了！
燈盡望著月月盡望著燈；
偶然的風娘姍姍地步來，
我想抱她喲卻撳痛了心。
十五，八，二十，夜半

26. Come On

Then I departed from you,
Then I departed from you in tears,
You are green leaves dyed with dew,
Like petals I fell to the ground.

Ah, you are my permanent love...
Like a cloud wave residing temporarily on the horizon.
Ah, come on, you, come on,
Like raindrops you run fast to me.
[August 21, 1926, midnight]

PART ONE: HEAVEN AND MAY

來吧

我便這樣地離了你,
我便這樣地離了帶淚的你,
你是染露的青葉子,
我便像那花瓣嚇落下了地。

啊你我底永久的愛……
像是雲浪暫時寄居在天海。
啊來吧你來吧來吧,
快像眼淚般的雨向我飛來。
　十五,八,二十一,夜半

27. Monologue of Love

You know, how could I
Put my book of jade into a storehouse of gold and silver!
As you know, when entering,
My purposeful heart again starts its purposeless journey.

Why, good fish　　　　　　　　　　　　　　　　　　　5
Do you have to swim alone in the surging waves of the deep?
Why, little sheep
Do you have to roam alone in the dens of lions, tigers, wolves
　　　and foxes?

Ah, if the person you love
Were wandering around traps more horrible than prisons,　10
If you are a noble person,
Could you remain calm like an unprotected lotus leaf being
　　　blown in the autumn wind?

Ah, you must have been tired and bored.
From the door of life to the door of death, you hold these joys
　　　and sorrows.
Ah, too many doors are opened,　　　　　　　　　　　15
Please do not ask where to go and beg an enemy for mercy.
[September 29, 1926, midnight]

PART ONE: HEAVEN AND MAY

愛的叮囑

你是知道了的,我怎願
我底玉石之書去走進那金銀之寶庫!
進去了時你是知道的,
我底有歸宿的心又入了無目的的路。

為什麼呢,好端端的魚
要獨自在氾濫洶湧的浪濤中去游泳?
為什麼呢,小小的羊兒
要獨自在獅洞虎穴狼窩狐窟前遊行?

啊使若你心愛的人兒
徘徊在比牢獄更可怕的陷阱之周圍,
你要是是有魂靈的人,
可仍像袒腹的荷葉臨著秋風般安泰?

啊已將疲憊而厭煩了。
從生之戶帶著快樂憂愁到死之門前。
啊辟開的門戶太多了,
請勿再問來去的道路而對仇讎乞憐。
十五,九,二九,夜半三時

28. Ex Dono Dei

Why is the whitewater ocean not white,
And ten million years of rain not wash clean heaven and earth?
Ah, I have seen darkness in the light--
Dirty skin attached to a clean body.

In sweet daytime or under sour, bitter moonlight,   5
I should kiss your lips and kiss your heart,
As in the deep valley I cry out and leap;
As in the fervent mountain springs I bathe and swim.
[no date]

PART ONE: HEAVEN AND MAY

恩賜

為什麼白水的海洋不是白的,
千萬年的雨嚇也洗不淨天地?
啊我曾在光明裏看見了黑暗——
穢汙的皮膚貼著乾淨的身體。

甜蜜的日中或是酸苦的月下,
我當吻著你的唇吻著你的心,
像在深奧的山谷裏呼號奔跳;
像在熱烈的澗泉裏沐浴游泳。
　(未記日期)

29. A Virgin Man Handling Women

A man has been living like a woman for twenty years long,
With love as the matchmaker, I expectedly married my own
    emotion,
It is just like loving the moon in order to mate a ghostly night.

The honey days of the newly wedded have been melted away
    in dreams,
The flood-like emotion has been seduced by that environ-
    ment,   5
And felt heavyhearted from delicate and weak actions.

Shame compelled me to build a house to hide myself,
Hide myself from being cursed by morality and maltreated by
    ethics,
I am someone of unyielding will and heart, a man of *lese-
    majeste*.

Ah, God, you are mine, and everything I have is yours, 10
You take care of my heavy-heart as you take Jesus in.
Jesus ever calls people to be like beasts of burden like him-
    self.
[undated]

PART ONE: HEAVEN AND MAY

童男的處女

二十年的男人生活做著女子過了,
因了愛的媒介嚇我竟嫁給了情感,
正像是戀著月而做那夜鬼的侶伴。

新婚的甜蜜的日子在睡夢中化去,
淫濫的情感又受了那環境的牽引,
在柔弱的動作的時期中私生煩悶。

羞恥逼迫著我自己造了屋子躲避,
躲避道德的詬罵以及禮教的殘凌,
我是個不屈志不屈心的大逆之人。

啊上帝你是我的我的一切是你的,
你像收留耶穌般收留我的煩悶吧,
他也曾以牛馬的資格叫人做牛做馬。
（未記日期）

30. Anch'io Sono Pittore!

I dream of standing by the statue of Apollo,
Around its rosy base sing little birds;
Sappho is playing her seven-string lute;
A.C. Swinburne is holding his fire-like passion;

John Keats is waking up and listening to the nightingale, 5
Back flow bitter tears in his sweet heart,
He is a shepherd lying in the grass,
The moon is trembling overhead to kiss him stealthily;

Ah, natural, artistic and musical,
Are verses written out of the soul of Paul Verlaine, 10
Ludwig van Beethoven has changed the new fashion,
Bringing green landscapes of the incredible;

Robert Burns is an honest and romantic farmer,
When you cry, your face still smiles,
Ah, joy is sweet and sorrow is not bitter, 15
Love in the country has its natural flavors;

Beside the dim lamp is Gorden Bottomley
Are you the devil fallen out of the heaven;
You put into a poem your flesh and your blood,
Can your demon be reborn on Earth too? 20

I cannot see Byron, Shelley and Shakespeare;
Nor Homer, the ancestor of poetry;
Goethe who loves his beloved friend's wife,

PART ONE: HEAVEN AND MAY

Has only been buried under time alone.
[no date]

我也是畫家！

我夢見立在愛普老的座旁，
玫瑰花的座周有小鳥歌唱；
莎茀撥彈著她七弦的仙琴；
史文朋抱著他火般的愛光；

濟慈正睡醒了癡聽著夜鶯，
倒流的淚染苦了甜蜜的心，
他是個牧羊兒在草上橫臥，
月娘戰戰兢兢地過來偷吻；

啊這自然的圖畫的音樂的，
是萬蕾的靈魂吐出的詩句，
彼多文的新風南的變形嚇，
又有著瓜綠的風景的神髓；

你這坦直多情的田夫彭思，
含淚時的你也帶著笑意，
啊快樂是甜的憂愁也不苦，
鄉村裏的愛有天然的風味；

豆般的煙燈邊的是包特蕾，
你是不是天上墮落的魔鬼；
你把你的肉你的血做了詩，
你這妖兒豈也在地下生產？

我不見拜倫雪萊莎士比亞；
也不見詩歌的祖宗荷馬；
那愛愛友的愛妻的哥德嚇，

PART ONE: HEAVEN AND MAY

只孤單單地壓在時光之下。
（未記日期）

31. Decadent Love

On heaven's bed lies a white cloud,
Accompanying him is not his lover;
Maybe urged by their lust,
They turned out to be hugging and kissing closely.

Ah, slept with this cloud,
And hung out tenderly with another,
In the color of the rhyme,
His soul has been destroyed.
[October 5, 1926, Shanghai]

PART ONE: HEAVEN AND MAY

頹加蕩的愛

睡在天床上的白雲，
伴著他的並不是他的戀人；
許是快樂的慫恿吧，
他們竟也擁抱了緊緊親吻。

啊和這一朵交合了，
又去和那一朵纏綿地廝混；
在這音韻的色彩裏，
便如此嚇消滅了他的靈魂。
十五，十，五，上海。

32. Under the Sunrise Building

Sounds of traffic, horns and spitting,
Curled-up smoke,
A woman's dress.

Crowded people move like winds and clouds,
Rush after rush of smelly flesh, blood   5
And sweat.

Roof, spire and clock,
Ten past ten o'clock;
Lights appeared together with stars in the sky.

I am at the crossroads,   10
Trembling with passions;
Thinking stealthily about a kiss.
[October 5, 1926 on the No. 1 trolley]

PART ONE: HEAVEN AND MAY

日昇樓下

車聲笛聲吐痰聲,
倏忽的煙形,
女人的衣裙。

似風動雲地人湧,
有肉腥血腥
汗腥的陣陣。

屋頂塔尖時辰鐘,
十點零十分;
星中雜電燈。

我在十字的路口,
戰顫著欲情;
偷想著一吻。
十五,十,五,一路電車中。

Part Two: Twenty-Five Poems in 1936

第二部分：《詩二十五首》1936年出版

PART TWO: TWENTY-FIVE POEMS

1. To a Poet

Should there appear a poet 100 years from now,
He will certainly not be like me, or like you;
With tenderness tightly binding his agile form,
He cannot tell if it is twilight or spring.

Alas, he would no longer remember me or you.   5
He would no longer miss our words and phrases:
In his eyes, I am a madman,
And you are a powdered and rouged flirt.

But there might also be an early morning after-dream awakening,
Smelling the fragrance of roses at the bedside;   10
He surprisedly pulls up his nightshirt,
Drawing out two copies of our poems from 100 years ago.
[First published in *Golden House Monthly* (Jinwu Yuekan) No. 3, 1929]

贈一詩人

假使一百年後再有個詩人,
他一定不像我,也不像你;
溫柔箍緊他靈活的身體,
他認不得這是黃昏這是春。

啊,他再不會記得我,記得你。
他再不會念我們的詞句;
在他眼睛裏,我是個瘋子,
你是個搽粉點胭脂的花癡。

但是也許有個夢後的早晨,
枕邊聞到了薔薇的香氣;
他竟會伸進他襯褥底裏,
抽出兩冊一百年前的詩本。

(首刊於1929年《金屋月刊》第3期)

PART TWO: TWENTY-FIVE POEMS

2. Xunmei's Dream

From the damask and absinthe green lotus flower,
A warm and tender dream appears, she nestles close to my
    soul;
As light as a cloud, I wonder,
Why does she not fly to the highest height or hide herself in a
    deep pool?
I still remember she once brought many gifts of hope,   5
And crept into pits of frustration; also, she has fallen into an
    affair
Which could startle a never-heavy-sleeping maiden awake,
Harming her from long baying of dogs to cock-crow:
But she seldom visited me here, because
She might not guess when I went to bed at night.   10
I love the sunshine to accompany my sleep, I hope
The nightingale will not disturb my weary state,
And perhaps at this empty moment, I can
Enter the gate of a garden, where all the flowers compose a
    song of colors and fragrance,   15
Making it a poem, to sing softly of the spring morning—
Even if a single string has been left on the lute, I do believe
She still will be able to play on it her scraps of lost sound,
(In the scraps lies the whole of her lingering feeling)
Even if you can block your ears,   20
Yet that single string has fire in it, she can actually
Fry you, boil you, burn down your hardness of iron and
    stone.
At the moment I must pull her down,
And help heaven to make her poet conceive.

In the flesh of the poet there is no foul seedling,   25
His embryo must naturally be a pure crystal,
In the future if he loves green leaves, then they will turn into
    jade,
If he loves red flowers, then they will turn into colorful coral:
Thus, God has his second son,
In the tranquil temple a new scripture will replace the old. 30
This is my hope, my dream: now, she is
Coming for sure; she takes me gently into
A forest, where I have been before, this is already
The edge of heaven, and almost the center of hell.
I see anew the twig I once kissed,   35
The lawn I once sat on, the flower shade where I lay.
I also once bathed myself in that spring water,
And the valley still embraces the sound of my first singing.
They all know me well, and they say, "Xunmei,
We have not seen you in the spring; in summer we do not see
    your trust;   40
In the autumn, we all long for your return;
The winter is gone, and still we have no news from you.
You know, heaven made us, it needs you to sing,
Without you, we have no gladness.
Come on, adorn us and say something grand for us,   45
Let others think we are immortals."
I heard, and immediately my blood boiled from head to toe,
My destiny is now clear, and in my control:
In the palace of the immortals it clearly is not mine to dwell.
Ah! I do not want to dream, but to wake, to wake!   50
[First published in *Poetry* No. 1, 1931]

PART TWO: TWENTY-FIVE POEMS

洵美的夢

從淡紅淡綠的荷花裏開出了
熱溫溫的夢,她偎緊我的魂靈。
她輕得像雲,我奇怪她為什麼
不飛上天頂或是深躲在潭心?
我記得她曾帶了滿望的禮物
躡進失意的被洞;又帶了私情
去驚醒了最不容易睡的處女,
害她從悠長的狗吠聽到雞鳴:
但是我這裏她不常來到,想是
她猜不准我夜晚上床的時辰。
我愛讓太陽伴了我睡,我希望
夜鶯不再攪擾我倦眠的心神,
也許乘了這一忽的空閒,我會
走進一個園門,那裏的花都能
把他們的色彩芬芳編成歌曲,
做成詩,去唱軟那春天的早晨——
就算是剩下了一根弦,我相信
她還是要彈出她屑碎的迷音,
(這屑碎裏面有更完全的纏綿)
任你能鎖住了你的耳朵不聽,
怎奈這一根弦裏有火,她竟會
煎你,熬你,燒爛你鐵石的堅硬。
那時我一定要把她摘采下來,
幫助了天去為她的詩人懷孕。
詩人的肉裏沒有汙濁的秧苗,
胚胎當然是一塊純粹的水晶,
將來愛上了綠葉便變成翡翠,
愛上了紅花便像珊瑚般妍明;

於是上帝又有了第二個兒子，
清淨的廟堂裏重換一本聖經。
這是我的希望，我的想；現在，她
真的來了；她帶了我輕輕走進
一座森林，我是來過的，這已是
天堂的邊沿，將近地獄的中心。
我又見到我曾經吻過的樹枝，
曾經坐過的草和躺過的花陰。
我也曾經在那泉水裏洗過澡，
山谷邊抱著我第一次的歌聲。
他們也都認識我，他們說：洵美，
春天不見你；夏天不見你的信；
在秋天我們都盼著你的歸來；
冬天去了，也還沒有你的聲音。
你知道，天生了我們，要你吟詠；
沒有了你，我們就沒有了歡欣。
來吧，為我們裝飾，為我們說誑，
讓人家當我們是一個個仙人。
我聽了，上下身的血立時滾沸，
我完全明白了我自己的運命：
神仙的宮殿絕不是我的住處。
啊，我不要做夢，我要醒，我要醒！
（首刊於 1931 年《詩刊》第 1 期）

3. Woman

I revere you, woman, I revere you just like
I revere a versicle of the Tang Dynasty—
Your warm and clear-cut tones of voice
Come to bind firmly my every sentence and word.

I suspect you, woman, I suspect you just like   5
I suspect a resplendent rainbow in the sky—
I do not know whether your red face is for me
Or still more for some other hot dream.
[First published in *Poetry* No. 2, 1931]

女人

我敬重你，女人，我敬重你正像
我敬重一首唐人的小詩——
你用溫潤的平聲乾脆的仄聲，
來捆縛住我的一句一字。

我疑心你，女人，我疑心你正像
我疑心一彎燦爛的天虹——
我不知道你的臉紅是為了我，
還是為了另外一個熱夢。
（首刊於1931年《詩刊》第2期）

4. A Little Poem

To you, I have never given a look at the picture on my heart;
There is something of you in it, even though it looks a little
 vague.

I will never forget you; though I become an immortal,
At heaven's gate, I would wait for you to go up together.

Though I fear to become a ghost, I would still endure the
 cold,   5
At the mouth of hell's cavern, I would still wait for your soul.

But now I just want to write you a little poem,
To tell you I am madder about you than I can say.
[First published in *Poetry* No. 2, 1931]

一首小詩

我沒曾給你看我心上的畫圖；
裏面有個你，雖然有些兒模糊。

我總忘不了你；假使我成了仙，
我要在天堂的門前等你上天。

那怕變了鬼我還是要耐了冷，
在地獄的洞口等著你的靈魂。

但是，現在我只能做一首小詩
對你說，我在想你想得發了癡。
（首刊於 1931 年《詩刊》第 2 期，原標題為"小詩一首"）

5. Seasons

When I see you the first time, you give me your heart,
Wherein lies a spring morn.

When I see you again, you give me your words,
Which reveal a passionate hot summer untold.

When I see you the third time, you give me your hand,   5
Wherein is concealed the fallen leaves of late autumn.

When I see you for the last time, you are a brief dream I had,
In which you still have a bevy of winter winds.
[First published in *Poetry* No. 2, 1931]

季候

初見你時你給我你的心，
裏面是一個春天的早晨。

再見你時你給我你的話，
說不出的是熾烈的火夏。

三次見你你給我你的手，
裏面藏著個葉落的深秋。

最後見你是我做的短夢，
夢裏有你還有一群冬風。
（首刊於 1931 年《詩刊》第 2 期）

PART TWO: TWENTY-FIVE POEMS

6. Voice

In the midst of a summer night's thunderstorm, a
Strange voice told me that I had taken the wrong path in my
    life.
The way I was going would not lead to a rainbow among
    white clouds,
And in the green leaves of willows, there would not be
Any shadow of peach flowers.   5
Then early this morning, an unknown envoy
Thrust an ordinary letter through the door crack;
Enchanting script signified a piece of ambiguous
News: she will bring me happiness, which will also be
Even more dreadful than a calamity.   10
I have no wish to become a firefly, even less
To throw my own flame into an eternal one;
I know that hungry eyes will always find their poisonous
Food, -- in fact, sometimes even God Himself cannot tell
The reason: when he forbids those with wings to fly;   15
Forbids those with passion to love;
Or forbids those with hopeful songs to lift their voices.

But a poem cannot end like this,
Just like God, it also has a never ending story.
She wanted me to reply, (but I could not think of any words),
                                                            20
So I said I love happiness and fear calamity;
After all, philosophy is not a virgin's expectation,
For a horror of white hairs cannot be compared with the
    bright red of a cherry;

She wanted me to speak my long-forgotten set phrases,
She wants me to trust her that a frail flower need not   25
Wither with the punishment of the seasons;
But I fear that yielding to sympathy will lay bare
My solemn hypocrisy, a naivete to be ruined.
I rub and put my right palm on the left,
Making a dull sound my answer.   30
At this point, I say that if there is some wine, it will help me
    to
Hand over an unexpected confession:
Though perhaps it is only a memorized poem,
An oft-heard word, or an oft-seen painting,
Yet they are all like arrows aimed at their target--   35
If shot, they will hit the bull's eye.
At this time, only Jesus can say to you, all
Solace, reward, and love hang on the nails of the cross.
This matter becomes troubling, and tears fall like raindrops,
Emotions blow like wind, making me lose my true self.   40
You may see for the first time soul and flesh
Speak words to each other which they dared not before.
Fortunately true sorrow is very often your guest,
You cannot avoid meeting him, just like people cannot avoid
    their souls,
Souls cannot avoid love, and love cannot avoid you.   45

When some commoner comes to your door,
Why do you welcome him as a miracle?
You have gone and matched a white dove with a black crow,
Mistaken a sparrow for a nightingale; you never ask him
    whether what he demands

PART TWO: TWENTY-FIVE POEMS

Is half of your suffering, or   50
Is devoted to you as a gift in full.

Alas, I hate the world for having you in it; without you,
The throb of longing must have proper restraint.
He would not lurk down dim alleys any longer,
Moving along grayish white walls, on his way to solve   55
An unsolvable riddle: thus to him boredom
Has no allure; sweated-out dreams
Will also ever be locked in oblivion's storehouse.
I hate you, because you approach me like wine splashed over
    a clean table:
Though I dare not catch fire,   60
Producing red, green, or yellow flowers,
Yet you cannot wait for that mad moment to come,
And just leave after carving some imprints engraved on my
    heart.
These imprints remain very deep, and seem made by some
    unknown
God's might, as though engraved by the thinnest gold needle
                                               65
In a place where they cannot be washed or worn away.
I do not believe there can be a second god in this world
Who can erase such traces so pure!
I hate you because you did not come to me and say,
All my first impressions of you were just my own fancy: 70
You never entered my heart, and never
There sowed a fertile flower's
Seed. I hate you, why did you tell me
That I should forget you, just like I have forgotten

Myself, regarding the twilight as beautiful as the morning. 75
Ah, fortunately I do understand the Moon, who says,
"Never have I smiled on you, that was a little wind
Blowing my veil; neither have I ever
Cried for you, that was spray out of a cold mist.
Nor have I ever once seen you, for my 80
Brightness is meant for the eyes of all under heaven.
You therefore must not blame me for disappointing you be-
    cause I have never
Required your care, sympathy and service.
You must also not blame me for treating you so coldly, be-
    cause I
Have never planned to socialize warmly. 85
Fire is yours, passion is yours, tenderness is
Yours, thus vexation is yours, too.
So you need not wait for me, for I have my own time to come
    and go:
When roosters crow, I hasten to sleep;
When birds sing in the evening, 90
I dress up to play, so be sure not to think
That my nightly comings and goings are just for you."
How pitiful is a man who has met an immortal, he invariably
    thinks
He can himself go to Heaven. He surely knows his wax wings
Will be melted in the brightness of the hot sunrays; he also
    surely knows 95
That strong winds have broken thousands of pairs
Of wings of iron and steel: but he can never help
His own desire to feel superior, so just as a meteor
Tends to crash into another planet, he will tend to come to

You. Suppose you are dreaming, when you hear   100
Some faraway voice calling your
Name--be careful, it must be him approaching you!
[First published in *Poetry Monthly*, No. 2, 1933; also appeared in *Tien Hsia Monthly*, Vol. 5, No.1, entitled as "Voice," trans. into English by Shao Xunmei and Harold Acton.]

聲音

夏夜在雷雨的中間,有一個
陌生的聲音對我說,我已走錯了
我要走的路,在白雲裏不能去找虹,
在楊柳的綠葉裏也不一定有
桃花的影子。
今早,不知名的天使
投進一封平常的信,從門縫裏:
迷醉的字體象徵一個含糊的
新聞,她給我幸福,她給我比幸福
更可怕的災害。
我不願做燈蛾,更不願
把自己的火去燒撲不滅的火;
我知道饑餓的眼睛會找到荼毒的
食糧,——原來上帝也有說不出
理由的時候;當他要禁止有翅膀的
飛,有情感的愛;有癡望的唱出
他自己都不曾預備著的歌聲。

但是詩不能就這樣地結束,
正如上帝也有他講不完的故事。
她要我答覆,(我想不出違心的話)
我說我喜歡幸福怕災害;
究竟哲學不是處女的期望,
白髮的恐怖不比櫻桃的豔紅,
她要我講出我遺忘了的成語,
她要我相信一朵嫩弱的花不用
季候的欺侮她自己會凋零;
但是,我怕,我怕讓同情揭穿了

PART TWO: TWENTY-FIVE POEMS

我莊嚴的虛偽，一個摧殘了的
天真。我把右手心貼著左手心，
一種單調的聲音做了我的回答。
這時候，我說，要是有酒，酒會
使我交出一篇料不到的供狀：
雖也許只是一首背熟的詩，
一個想熟的字，一張看熟的畫；
可是他們都會像箭頭瞄準了
箭靶，一射就射中最裏面的一點。
這時候，只有耶穌會對你說，一切的
安慰，報酬和愛都在那一支釘上。
事情就會鬧大，眼淚會像雨，
情感會像風，自己會沒有主張。
你便會第一次見到靈魂和肉體
各自說出各自不敢說的話。
好在憂愁是你家常住的客，
你少不掉他，正如人少不掉靈魂，
靈魂少不掉愛，愛少不掉你。

為什麼平凡也會踏進你的門，
你款待他像是款待一個奇跡？
你竟然把白鴿去配烏鴉，你把
麻雀當夜鶯；你不問他所要求的
是不是你痛苦的半份，或是
來對你貢獻一顆完整的禮物。

啊，我恨這世上有你，沒有你
情感的跳動就有了一定的分寸。
他不再會在那條幽暗的狹弄裏，
那壁灰白的高牆邊，去解答一種

解答不出的啞謎：煩悶對於他
就沒有了誘惑：出汗的夢
也就永遠封鎖進遺忘的倉庫。
我恨你，因為你像酒精潑上光淨的
桌子般來到我這裏：我雖然不敢
燃上火，造成紅的，綠的或是黃的花，
但是你卻不等那瘋癲的時刻到來，
竟在我心上留了片印子走了。
這印子留得深，像是用了不知
那一個神的力，把最細的金針
鏽在不能洗滌也不能磨滅的
地方。我不信還會有第二個神
能為我抹去這一個純潔的痕跡！
我恨你不走來對我說，我所有的
你的印象原是我自己的幻想：
你從沒有到過我心裏，更沒有
在我心裏撒過一粒會開花的
種子。我恨你為什麼不對我說，
我應當把你忘掉，像我忘掉
我自己，當黃昏長得像早晨般美麗。
啊，幸虧月亮的話我懂得，她說：
我從沒有對你笑，那是小風
帶動了我的面紗：我也從沒有
對你下淚，那是冷霧裏的水花。
我也從沒有看過你一次，我的
光明是為了天下人的眼睛。
你不用怪我辜負你，我從沒有
需要你的愛護，憐惜和侍候。
你也不用怪我冷淡你，因為我
從沒有預備著熱烈的酬應。

PART TWO: TWENTY-FIVE POEMS

火是你的，癡是你的，溫柔是
你的，那懊惱就得由你收受。
你更不用等著我，我的來去
有我自己的時候：雄雞的啼號
會催我睡眠，晚上小鳥的歌唱
又會催我梳裝，你千萬不用想
我的朝暮的來去又是為了你。
可憐一個見過仙人的，他總想
自己上天。他明知道蜜臘的羽翼
會化盡在火熾的日光裏；他明知道
雲邊的大風曾吹斷過幾千萬對
鋼鐵的翅膀；但是他總制不住
欲望的超升，像是一顆隕石
要趨向另一個星球，他要趨向
你。——假使你在夢中，聽得有
一個遙遠的聲音在喚著你的
名字，留心，這便是他在走近！

（首刊於 1933 年《詩篇》月刊第 2 期。1937 年邵洵美與 Harold Acton 合譯此詩，刊於 *Tien Hsia*（《天下》）月刊第 5 卷第 1 期，題為"Voice"。）

7. Nature's Command

Nature's command, the power to choose is hers.
As long as she is willing, she can put her heart
Sky-high amidst a big bird's wings,
She can also follow the sharp-eyed hawk
Shooting a restless arrow; she can also   5
Let the white dove bear her to smoothly travel, travel
To the high clouds, where she proudly overlooks
The group of friends who once madly courted her.
But she wants to wait. I don't know if she is
Waiting for them to be sad, to set off   10
In the third winter her cold good-bye!
I was already aware that her crisp decision will be broken into
    pieces that
Can't resist the strike from the north wind.
Because she can sing, sing until the nightingale turns dumb;
Because she has a pair of eyes that cannot look far.   15
Her stare will make the peacock ashamed to color up.
But what most people love is her quietness,
Loneliness like a faint island in the mist five miles away:
No wind within her borders, I almost
Don't believe the river will flow around her.   20
If in the morning, in the earliest morning, we see
The dewdrops covered her with a transparent dream,
We will be afraid of her delicate body
Unable to embrace it, shedding light sweat;
But who would dare to pick this heart-throbbing   25
Scenery? Ah, I would like to have a single instrument of tor-
    ture

That can bind her, which had better be a yoke of iron and
    steel,
Holding fast her hands, feet, eyes and lips,
Shutting her down in a heavenly prison for thirty-three days,
So her voice would never pass on to the world.   30
Usually she was feeding on unusual grasses and grains;
In feeding her, are you preparing a food for the gods?
Maybe she is willing to stand up hunger and thirsty for it, but
What is the significance of this hunger and thirsty? You can't
    lie by using
A bamboo cage as a gold palace hall;   35
Nor can you fool her with a small goblet of syrup for
Honey from Corsican grapes.
Because she is just a naive little bird,
Who doesn't know her beloved will lie to her.
The whole thing cannot deceive me, so telling lies should 40
Have a limit. You can tell the vain phoenix that
You have tens of thousands of peonies, you can say that
You have a sun to serve as her mirror when she makes up
    from dawn to dusk;
You can say to a tough crow that you have a
Soft bed which is three hundred times warmer than a mag-
    pie's nest: 45
Pain is their birthmark, God promises you.
But you don't have to lie to her; you have to allow her
To enjoy the spring breeze twice as much as possible,
To let her understand that the vast universe has not
Treated her unfairly, and never tires of her chant.   50
[Published in *Poetry Monthly* No. 1, 1933]

自然的命令

自然的命令，選擇的權柄是她的。
只要她願意，她可以安置她的心
在大鵬鳥的翅膀中間飛上青天，
她也可以跟隨最眼快的老鷹
射那不肯放鬆的一箭；她也可以
讓白鴿帶了她平穩地旅行，旅行
到頂高的雲端，再驕傲地俯瞰
那一群曾瘋癲地追逐她的朋友。
可是她要等，我不懂她是不是
要等人家憂愁的長成，來襯托
第三個冬天，她一聲冰冷的再會！
我早就明白她這一個鬆脆的決定
受不住北風的打擊馬上就破碎。
因為她能唱，唱到夜鶯變啞吧；
因為她有一雙看不遠的眼睛
會看得孔雀羞慚地把彩屏收起。
可是最叫人憐愛的，是她的幽靜，
孤獨像五裏外輕霧裏隱約的島嶼：
在她的疆界裏沒有風，我幾乎
不相信江水會在她的周圍流動。
要是在早晨，在最早的早晨，我們看
露珠罩住她用一網透明的夢，
我們就會怕這一段嬌弱的身體，
要經不起擁抱，淌出淡味的汗；
可是誰又敢挑破這張心跳的
風景？啊，我單願有殘忍的刑具
能加上她，更好是鋼鐵的枷鎖，
枷鎖住她的手，腳，眼睛和嘴唇，

PART TWO: TWENTY-FIVE POEMS

把她關閉進三十三天上的牢獄,
叫她的聲音永遠傳不到人間。
本來喂哺她不能用平常的草穀;
侍候她,你可預備著神仙的食糧?
也許她自願忍受這饑渴,可是
這饑渴有什麼名目?你不能用
竹編的籠子騙她是金鑄的宮殿;
你不能用一小觚糖水騙她是
打蜜鐵嶺島上帶來的葡萄漿。
因為她只是一頭天真的小鳥,
不知道愛她的會對她說謊。
事情全瞞不了我,講假話總得
有個分寸。你可以對虛榮的鳳凰
說你有幾千幾萬朵牡丹,說你有
一面太陽可以早晚照著她梳裝;
你可以對強悍的烏鴉說你有比
喜鵲的窩巢三百倍溫軟的床鋪:
苦楚是他們的名分,上帝許你。
可是你總不應當騙她,你得讓
她儘量地享受兩次春風的撫拂,
讓她明白這老大的宇宙從沒有
待虧她,從沒有厭倦她的吟詠。
(首刊於1933年《詩篇》月刊第1期)

8. Heaven and Earth

Please pardon me this empty, wanton stubbornness, immortal
    goddess.
Awake and asleep I invariably see you; the reason is
I long ago engraved your image into a model,
And marked it in countless imprints on my soul.
I sing your praises, no matter whether you hear or not,   5
Crying out exactly like a midday's cock crow;
For me, every single second is half a day,
Every single second moreover can uplift my voice.
But I never expect you to come down from heaven—
A thunderbolt disrupting all creation.   10
I just wish casually, that one day in spring,
When dutiful people are cheerful by keeping themselves busy,
A breeze can calmly and collectedly deliver a message,
Saying heaven and earth may ultimately join together.
[First published in *Poetry Monthly* No. 2, 1933]

PART TWO: TWENTY-FIVE POEMS

天和地

請原諒我這荒誕的固執,仙人。
醒時睡時我總看見你;原因是
我早把你的形象刻成了印子,
打上無數的印花在我的靈魂。
我對你的頌揚,不管你聽不聽,
準確地喊叫著像正午的雞啼;
為我每一秒鐘就是一個晝時,
每一秒鐘又會加高我的嗓音。
我並不希望你會從天上下來——
一個霹靂要驚動一切的事物。
我但願不經意地在一個春天,
當人們自己忙著自己的歡快,
小風能不動聲色地送個消息,
就說天和地終有一天會接連。
(首刊於1933年《詩篇》月刊第2期)

9. Undisputed Faith

Do not suspect me unduly, my friend.
Sincerely I desire to decorate this wall
With too many masterpieces,
Astonishing the owner of the house to see
Frequent unexpected transformations in their frames.   5
I mean neither to conceal nor to flaunt my collection,
But I know well that in the air of the changing seasons
New colors should be employed at all times:
On hilltops and treetops,
Spring cannot yearn for the clothes of winter;   10
Like white snow, it takes no fixed
Forms, but it enjoys freedom in its
Maximum. It can never cut relations with
Or elude the immortal gods'
Control and commands. She is a   15
Willing slave, which you know very well.
Occasionally, I will hang some seductive
Paintings on the wall to make the house owner overly elated,
Believing the universe has betrayed him in his
Bedroom; he soon forgot   20
That emotionless face outside the window--
Poor guy, he is unwilling to give up his historic
Honor. Occasionally I will replace them with common sketches,
Because the instant happiness runs faster
Than the time spent, which will   25
Halt that interval's joy, and this you must
Ponder in lonely silence; but

This does not mean that life is death,
Because death is after all a concession
To a postponed bill, and you may borrow   30
Divine power or man's power to persuade
Death to give you more time to pay it.
I do believe it is possible,
Otherwise the god of death too could feel
The dullness of his authority. Sometimes, I even think   35
I should hang some works of the greatest purity on the wall,
Without assigned themes and without titles,
Only the building of lines and colors;
This building may have some meaning, but
Their creator cares little about whether his   40
Results are successful or not.
This is the test of truth which you can
Drag out to dream up any illusion.
My friend, my painstaking efforts might
Make you feel inconvenient and superfluous;   45
But this is all what I can do:
Try my best to offer the artificial as solace to the natural.
[First published in *Poetry Monthly* No. 3, 1933]

不變的信念

不要過分地懷疑我，朋友。
誠心地我要裝飾這牆壁，
但是我有太多的名作
會使主人驚異這鏡框裏
時常有不可預言的變換。
我並沒有想要遮隱或炫耀，
但是我明白在季節更替的
空氣裏，色調要隨時有
新的配置；像是山頭和樹頂
春天不能留戀冬天的衣裳；
像是白雪，它沒有固定的
形式，但是它自由在一個
最大的範圍裏。它決不會，
也從沒有躲避仙神的
駕馭和使遣。它是一個
會心的奴隸，你該明白。
我時常會放進誘惑的
圖畫，使主人過度地興奮，
使他以為宇宙在他的
臥室裏失了節；他早忘卻
窗帷外那只鐵板的面孔——
可憐它不願放棄它歷史的
尊嚴。我又時常會放進
平淡的速寫，因為跑得
比時光更快的，還有
剎那間的歡樂，這個，你須在
冷寂中去回味；但是，
這並不說生命便是死，

PART TWO: TWENTY-FIVE POEMS

因為死究竟是一片容許
延宕的賬單，你可以借了
神的力或是人的力去關說，
要他寬限些時日再索取。
我相信這事情的可能，
否則死神也會感覺到
他權威的單調。我又時常會
放進一些最純粹的作品，
沒有指定也沒有名目，
只是線條和色彩的建築；
這建築也許有意義，但是
創造者從沒有顧慮到它的
結果是失敗或是成功。
這是真理的試探，你可以
借名來捏造出多少幻象。
朋友，我的苦心，也許會
使你感到麻煩和多餘；
但這是我所能做的一切：
儘量地把人工去安慰天然。
（首刊於 1933 年《詩篇》月刊第 3 期）

10. Self

I come to know it is myself, endlessly counting in silence
In the mouth of the nightingale these 365 days:
These pointless printed marks.

It is not the first time that I suspect that God has moved the
    wrong
Beads on an abacus, resulting in an inaccurate sum;   5
I know there is a scripture hall on one side of the inkstone.

Tidal water also evades the moon, so why
Must they turn into tears and make the goddess cry?
Yet she finds it impossible to fill full the ravine.

Now it should be your time to recall: 10
Immoveable is the lonely island in the middle of the river,
She has once been raped, body and soul.
[First published in *Poetry Monthly* No. 1, 1933]

PART TWO: TWENTY-FIVE POEMS

自己

我認識這是我自己,默數著
夜鶯嘴裏三百六十五個日子:
這些不適用的鉛印的記號。

已不是一次,我疑心上帝撥錯了
算盤珠,結果是不準確的答數;
我知道墨硯的半邊有一間經堂。

潮水也會逃避月亮,為什麼
一定要變成眼淚叫天神哭?
但是,她發現了填不滿的溝壑。

現在應當是你能回想的時候:
搬不動是江心裏一座孤島,
她曾經被姦汙,身體和靈魂。
(首刊於 1933 年《詩篇》月刊第 1 期。)

11. Whom Do You Take Me For?

Whom do you take me for?
Am I a prodigal son, a moneygrubber, a scholar;
Do I want to be an official, or perhaps a hero with no fear of
    death?
You are wrong, you are entirely wrong;
I am a born poet!   5

I love gold because of her gleaming color;
I love a pearl because of her shining rays;
I love women because they are all poems;
Ah, everything under heaven I love,
Only if it is uncommon.   10

Yet, there are times when
The most common soap bubble, meow from a cat,
Or tadpole swimming in a ditch,
Also make me intoxicated and palpitating,
Which makes me forget that I am a poet myself.   15

Do I make soap bubbles into rainbows,
Do I make meowing into the laughter of spring,
Do I make tadpoles into women's eyes?
I do not know, I do not know at all;
You have to ask that poet who does not speak deceit. 20
[First published in *Golden House Monthly*, No. 11, 1930]

PART TWO: TWENTY-FIVE POEMS

你以為我是什麼人?

你以為我是什麼人?
是個浪子,是個財迷,是個書生,
是個想做官的,或是不怕死的英雄?
你錯了,你全錯了;
我是個天生的詩人。

我愛金子為了她燦爛的色彩;
我愛珠子為了她晶亮的光芒;
我愛女人為了她們都是詩;
啊,天下的一切我都愛,
只要是不同尋常。

但是,有的時候,
極平常的一個肥皂泡,一聲貓叫,
或是在田溝裏游泳的蝌蚪,
也會使我醉,使我心跳,
使我把我自己是個詩人忘掉。

是不是把肥皂泡當作了虹,
把貓叫當作了春的笑聲,
把蝌蚪當作了女人的眼睛?
我不知道,我全不知道;
你得去問那個不說謊的詩人。
(首刊於 1930 年《金屋月刊》第 11 期。)

12. Peony

The peony also knows death
But her red is like that of a virgin,
> And her shaking is like that of a wanton woman,
> Driving you and me mad in broad daylight,
> And in black night to dream.

What she lacks is her fragrance:
Although she once appeared in verses and gave them some
  sweet savor,
> And mixes tears with trickery,
I will never forget that moist flesh,
> That deeply flushed skin,
That tipsy feeling of tightly coiled release.
[First published in *Golden House Monthly* No. 11, 1930]

PART TWO: TWENTY-FIVE POEMS

牡丹

牡丹也是會死的
但是她那童貞般的紅
　淫婦般的搖動,
　盡夠你我白日裏去發瘋,
　黑夜裏去做夢。

少的是香氣:
雖然她亦曾在詩句里加進些甜味,
　在眼淚裏和入些詐欺,
但是我總忘不了那潮潤的肉,
　那透紅的皮,
那緊擠出來的醉意。
（首刊於 1930 年《金屋月刊》第 11 期）

13. In the Eye of a Traveller

Tenderness lies beside the pillow in your own home,
In the eye of a traveler are endless uncertainties,
Every strange face is a panic;
A nameless bird sings a song for me,
But I also think her song is to mock me from the east. 5

There are some soothing hands around my neck,
And I pay good money in exchange for their favors,
Even in the mirror there were two different pairs of eyes;
I fear that once the fragrant rose has been sucked by a bee,
The worst is that the soul comes to know its sweetness there-
    after.   10
[First published in *Golden House Monthly* No. 4, 1929]

PART TWO: TWENTY-FIVE POEMS

出門人的眼睛

溫柔匍伏在自己家裏的枕旁，
出門人的眼中是數不盡的渺茫，
每一隻陌生人的面孔是一種恐慌；
不知名的鳥兒便是對了我歌唱，
我也當是在嘲笑我來自東方。

也有繾綣的手圈住我的項頸，
我也盡把金錢去換他們的恩情，
鏡子裏也有過兩對兩樣的眼睛；
我怕異香的玫瑰雖讓小蜂吸吮，
遭殃的是那嘗到甜味的靈魂。
（首刊於 1929 年《金屋月刊》第 4 期）

14. I Dare not Go to Heaven

I dare not go to heaven, I dare not go to heaven,
Up in heaven there are many beauties with prematurely white
    hair,
If you invite me to go, I will go, but I am afraid
Of finding my beauty become old.

Though I have deeply inhaled the flower's fragrance,   5
And once savored sweet stories,
But the most frightening are the most delicate two petals,
Calling me to pour out my life within their ripple.

I want to erect a building of micaceous stone,
On which locks of hair have been engraved;   10
I want these clingy threads of sirens
To no longer be able to tie up my soul.

In the court of heaven where no one becomes old,
I am not afraid that Buddha demands me to act serious;
I am thus afraid, I also wonder, why   15
Every single fairy maiden is so young.
[First published in *Athens* No. 1, 1929]

PART TWO: TWENTY-FIVE POEMS

我不敢上天

我不敢上天,我不敢上天,
天上有不少白了的紅顏,
你要我去,我便去,怕只怕
找到了的心兒又要不見。

雖然我已經聞過了花香,
甜蜜的故事我也曾品嘗,
但是可怕那最嫩的兩瓣,
盡叫我一世在裏面蕩漾。

我要造個雲母石的建築,
上面刻著一束束的髮束;
我要叫這些纏人的妖絲
不再能將我的靈魂捆縛。

在這年歲老不了的天廷,
我不怕菩薩要我扮正經;
我就怕,我又奇怪,為什麼
一個個的仙女都很年輕。
(首刊於 1929 年《雅典》第 1 期)

15. Lines of Verse Never Imagined

Wine is for people to drink, my friend, so people drink wine,
Golden yellow, emerald green, even whiter than white jade;
All these wines in your gut, flowing in your blood vessels—
Dancing as hard as dancing girls, swimming as fast as small fishes;

Move gracefully, drink elegantly, roll over and over, I understand the message of wine: 5
"Do not forget that today is more dear than tomorrow, and has more care.
If you want something, you can get it when you are drunk,
For there, gold is not hard to dig, and fresh flowers can be picked.

"There, the late night is not dark, and the sun never becomes red;
There, we exceed sweet dreams of happiness we may have dreamed or not;   10
There, time runs more leisurely;
There, sorrow puts on a happy mask.

Come on, my friend, at once let us go there together,
One cup, two cups, three cups, and you won't know or care who you are;
Then, you, my friend, then you,   15
Seem to think of a line of verse which you never imagined before.

[First published in *Golden House Monthly* No. 1, 1929]

PART TWO: TWENTY-FIVE POEMS

永遠想不到的詩句

酒是人喝的,朋友,人便得喝酒,
金黃的,翠綠的,連比白玉更白的都有;
經過了腸子,便打血管裏面走,——
一個個舞女在跳舞,一條條魚兒在遊;

嫋動,輕送,翻湧,我懂得酒的話,
莫忘了今天比明天更值得寶貴,牽掛。
要什麼東西不妨到醉裏去拿,
那裏有掘不到的黃金,采不到的鮮花;

那裏的深夜不黑,太陽不煊紅;
那裏有我們做過的與沒做過的歡夢;
那裏的時光奔跑得比較從容;
那裏的憂愁的確有一隻快樂的面孔。

來吧,朋友,我們趕快同去那裏,
一杯,兩杯,三杯,管叫你把自己忘記;
這時候的你,朋友,這時候的你
便好像想到了句永遠想不到的詩句。
(首刊於 1929 年《金屋月刊》第 1 期)

16. The Voice Sent by the Wind

I do not believe, I do not believe, this voice sent by the wind;
The first reason is that I remain as I was when young.
Do you notice that my lips are the same color as of cherries,
Still tightly wrapping my pair of white jade-like teeth?

In this deep red bedroom lies, oh! a sleeping beauty,   5
Rosy cheeks, rosy upper body and lower body;
Friend, though you are as patient as a real gentleman,
I am very afraid that her little tongue will hook you in.

Do not mention my straight nose, or my expressive eyebrows;
Do not compare my eyes to shining stars in the sky;   10
Do not compare my dimples to snares;
Do not compare my hair to black clouds or yellow gold.

Do not say my hands are like bamboo shoots in spring, and my
    feet like red water-chestnuts;
Do not say my breast is like a happy fawn's;
Do not say that my liveliness is all you need;   15
Just hush, calm down and look at my immortal godlike stature.

One hundred souls, one hundred souls will be degraded for me;
One hundred pairs of wings, one hundred pairs of wings will
    be broken for me;
The fire in my belly can even burn you to death, yet you still
    come to me for shelter;
Set no maze for you, and do not worry about you not going on
    this journey.   20

PART TWO: TWENTY-FIVE POEMS

Alas, who said that there can indeed be a second monstrous seductress,
Daring to seize what I have in my hands, below my waist, and enslave me?
Away, away, cease using your honeyed words to make a sweet palace,
I do not believe, I do not believe this voice sent by the wind.
[First published in *Sphinx* (Shihou) No. 7, 1928]

風吹來的聲音

我不相信，我不相信，這風吹來的聲音，
第一，我現在仍是和以前同樣地年青。
你不看見嗎，與櫻桃一般顏色的嘴唇，
仍將我這兩行白玉的牙齒包得緊緊？

在這紅紅的臥房裏，啊，還睡著個美人，
血霞色的臉兒，血霞色的上身與下身；
朋友嚇，盡你有幾千個柳下惠的耐忍，
怕難逃，怕難逃，這小小舌尖兒的鉤引。

不講我端正的鼻子；或是能言的眉心；
也用不到將閃爍的星星比我的眼睛；
也用不到將這一顆顆酒渦去比陷阱；
也用不到將我的頭髮去比烏雲，黃金；

也用不到說我的手像春筍，腳向紅菱；
也用不到說我的胸脯像小鹿般歡欣；
也用不到說我的活潑能使你們盡情；
且靜一靜心，看我整個兒的似仙似神。

一百個靈魂，一百個靈魂要為我沉淪；
一百對羽翼，一百對羽翼要為我折盡。
火熾的心窩，你便燒死，你也得來投奔；
不必布什麼迷陣，怕你不走這條路程。

啊，誰說人間真會有第二個怪物妖精，
敢將我手掌中的，裙腰下的，囚奴占侵？
去，去，休將你的口蜜造出甜香的宮廷，

PART TWO: TWENTY-FIVE POEMS

我不相信,我不相信這風吹來的聲音。
(首刊於 1928 年《獅吼》復活號半月刊第 7 期)

17. If I Were Also Like an Immortal

If I were also like an immortal,
I would change into a horse or an elephant;
I would grow a pair of wings on my back,
I would turn into the most beautiful phoenix.

I would make women feel jealousy,   5
I would make women know modesty;
So if some suitor courts her,
She will not sleep in the clouds any more.

If I were also like an immortal,
I would change into a horse or an elephant;   10
I would scribble on myself in gold;
I would turn into an iron-hearted idol.

Then if some weeping women begged me for pity,
I would not alter my countenance;
Nor would I hold back my sweat and tears any more--15
Instead, I would compose some poetry and respectfully offer
    it to them.
[First published in *Golden House Monthly* No. 12, 1930]

PART TWO: TWENTY-FIVE POEMS

假使我也和神仙一樣

假使我也和神仙一樣,
會把自己來變馬變象;
我要在背上生對羽翼,
變一隻最美麗的鳳凰。

我要叫女人看了妒忌,
我要叫女人知道謙虛;
以後有男子向她求愛,
不再把自己睡在雲裏

假使我也和神仙一樣,
會把自己來變馬變象;
我要在身上塗些金色;
變一個鐵心腸的偶像。

那時有女人哭著乞憐,
我便不再會改動聖顏;
也不再忍了汗忍了淚,
做了詩向她們去呈獻。
（首刊於 1930 年《金屋月刊》第 12 期）

18. Green Dies from the Banana

Green dies from the banana, red dies from the rose,
I will no longer be enamored of colors;
Maybe there will yet be a day or a night,
When she will lead me back to the realm of yesterday's dream.

If raindrops from the sky had the chance to fly again, 5
I could gather the stars and the moon as a present for you;
The only pity is that the white dove has become aged,
He does not want to tease the rosy clouds any more.
[First published in *Golden House Monthly* No. 4, 1929]

PART TWO: TWENTY-FIVE POEMS

綠逃去了芭蕉

綠逃去了芭蕉，紅逃去了薔薇，
我再不能在色彩中找到醉迷；
也許會有一個白日或是黑夜，
她將我領回昨天的夢的國裏。

假使落下地的雨點再會高飛，
我一定能采了星和月來贈你；
只是可憐的白鴿已上了年紀，
他再不想去逗引霞雲的歡喜。
（首刊於 1929 年《金屋月刊》第 4 期）

19. A Dead Chinese Lute

This is a dead Chinese lute,
He cannot sing and cannot speak any more;
He thus has no story to tell,
He thus does not think of matching gifted scholars with pretty
    lasses;

He has long since become old, become old,   5
His withered throat does not make ardent tones;
Some sighing breath, some choking coughs,
And then it is time for him to keep silence.

He has no sweet news to tell,
He is afraid that you recognize his sad face.   10
Leave him alone and do not interrupt him again,
He has long been a dead Chinese lute.
[First published in *Golden House Monthly* No. 3, 1929]

PART TWO: TWENTY-FIVE POEMS

死了的琵琶

這是一隻死了的琵琶,
他再不能歌唱再不能說話;
他已沒有要講的故事,
他已不想把才子去配嬌娃;

他早已是老了的,老了,
枯喉裏早沒有熱烈的音調;
幾聲歎息又幾聲嗆咳,
這便是他靜默的時候已到。

他已沒有甜蜜的消息;
他怕你們把他的苦顏認識。
饒了他吧,莫再去撥彈,
這一隻琵琶早已是死了的。

(首刊於 1929 年《金屋月刊》第 3 期)

20. Serpent

Below the steps of a palace, on the tiles of a temple roof,
You let hang the most delicate part of your body--
Just like a woman's half-loosened girdle
Awaiting the male's quivering bravery.

I do not know which of my lips your blood-red forked tongue
                                                      5
Intends to sting?
They are both ready, ready for the bite,
Which gives them twice the elation at the same time!

I cannot forget your uncatchable slipperiness,
Which polishes your many joints: 10
I know that in pleasure there is pain,
And I know better that in the ice-cold there is fire.

Ah, I wish you could use the rest of your length
To come and coil tightly around my loose body,
When the bell sound creeps into the mosquito net in the prayer
    house,   15
Warmth will fill the embroidered quilt in the cold palace.
[First published in *Vox* (Shengse) No. 1, 1931, a Chinese-English pictorial monthly]

PART TWO: TWENTY-FIVE POEMS

蛇

在宮殿的階下,在廟宇的瓦上,
你垂下你最柔嫩的一段——
好像是女人半松的褲帶
在等待著男性的顫抖的勇敢。

我不懂你血紅的叉分的舌尖
要刺痛我那一邊的嘴唇?
他們都準備著了,準備著
這同一個時辰裏雙倍的歡欣!

我忘不了你那捉不住的油滑
磨光了多少重疊的竹節:
我知道了舒服裏有傷痛,
我更知道了冰冷裏還有火熾。

啊,但願你再把你剩下的一段
來箍緊我箍不緊的身體,
當鐘聲偷進雲房的紗帳,
溫暖爬滿了冷宮稀薄的繡被!
(首刊於 1931 年《聲色》雜誌第 1 期)

21. Love Looted

Take it, please, because it is stolen from you.

Whoever visits the flowering shrubs,1 will he not take home some fragrance,
Some intoxication, some vague perception, even some illusions?
Last night I took back something poetic from the poet,
Today I have taken back some stolen love from my lover.　5

Like two or three petals from the white rose,
Delicate and slippery, be careful of dizzy eyes from watching them:
This petal carries many thousand kilos of advice and consolation;
That petal carries many thousand kilos of jealousy and resentment;

Now for the last petal, long incomplete,　　　　　　　　10
Maybe because of moist tears or licking?
Ah, I give them back to you, for I fear they will become yellow and withered,
Because they are parted from you, the source of life.
[First published in *Golden House Monthly* No. 5, 1929]

---

[1] The term "flowering shrubs" (*hua cong*) is also a Chinese idiom for "world of debauchery."

PART TWO: TWENTY-FIVE POEMS

情贓

拿去吧,這是從你那裏偷來的。

去過花叢的誰不帶回一點花香,
一點醉,一點縹緲,再是一點幻象?
昨夜在詩人那裏帶回了些詩意,
今天在情子那裏帶回了些情贓。

像是白薔薇的花瓣兒兩片三片,
又嫩又滑的,留心看暈了你的眼:
這一片有幾千萬斤的勸告,安慰;
那一片有幾千萬斤的醋意,怨嗔;

再有最後的一片,早已殘缺不全,
是淚兒濕化了,還是經了舌兒舔?
啊,還了你吧,我怕白花瓣會變黃,
他們已離了你,離了生命的源泉。
(首刊於 1929 年《金屋月刊》第 5 期)

22. On the Top of Zijinshan

I am not climbing vines, nor striding on clouds,
I am sent up to the highest peak by the symbol of power,
Where I survey from the east to the west,
Looking down from on high over the movements of all creatures;
The whole city of Nanjing is just like a lotus leaf,   5
Xuanwu Lake is just like a dewdrop on it:
If this scenery could be put into a short poem,
Then let us try to describe nature's quiet solitude.
I look further, and see the furthermost haze,
I dislike white clouds not clear enough, or sleepy   10
Too-red sunshine; I look at the moon again, half awaking,
And am afraid she thinks she is still dreaming.
Ah, the greatest creature is man, today I come to understand this,
That God make many things for man to critique.
[First published in *Poetry Monthly* No. 1, 1933]

PART TWO: TWENTY-FIVE POEMS

在紫金山

我沒有攀著藤,也沒有跨著雲,
力的象徵送我上最高的峰巔,
我可以打最東邊看到最西邊,
俯視著幾百千種生靈的動靜;
整個的南京原來像一張荷葉,
玄武湖像是荷葉上一顆露珠:
要是這光景可以寫成首短詩,
那麼就試這一幕自然的冷寂。
我再看,看到了最遠處的朦朧,
我嫌那白雲不夠透明,疲倦的
太陽太紅;再看那月亮,一半醒,
怕她自己還以為自己在做夢?
啊,最偉大的是人,我今天明白,
上帝造這許多東西給他批評。
(首刊於 1933 年《詩篇》月刊第 1 期)

23. Come down to the Countryside

Come down to the countryside --
In front of a yellow cow
A bowl of white rice.

Come down to the countryside --
Climb up a mountain at daybreak,
And come down at dusk.

Come down to the countryside --
Old people in the country
Are ageless.

Come down to the countryside --
A young country girl
Plants green vegetables skillfully.

Come down to the countryside --
If you cannot become a poet,
Come down to the countryside.
[First published in *Golden House Monthly* No. 12, 1930]

PART TWO: TWENTY-FIVE POEMS

到鄉下來

到鄉下來——
黃牛的跟前
一碗白飯。

到鄉下來——
天明了上山,
暗了下山。

到鄉下來——
鄉下的老人
沒有年歲。

到鄉下來——
鄉下的少女
會種青菜。

到鄉下來——
做不成詩人,
到鄉下來。
(首刊於 1930 年《金屋月刊》第 12 期)

24. An Old Tree of Two Hundred Years

In front of that temple, near the water, there is an old tree,
Bare crown and wrinkled skin,
With widespread arms he looks far into the distance,
Seeming to tell of his own depression long buried in his heart.

Two hundred years ago, he set his root here,   5
Never moving again,
He has witnessed the wall building of every village,
He has witnessed the painting of every village house;

He has witnessed hundreds of boys and girls,
Sleeping around the arms of mothers in childhood,   10
Breast-sucking, crying, smiling, opening and shutting their eyes,
Soon they leave their mothers to do the fieldwork.

When the boys grow up, the girls become beauties,
They date under the shade of the tree,
He forgets his plow and hoe in the field,   15
She forgets her dishes and rice in the pot.

"I will ride on the cow's back blowing my flute,
You sit by the bamboo fence sewing summer clothes,
Spring will climb up the tree crowning the hill,
Do not forget to meet me in the backyard tonight."   20

"I will sit by the bamboo fence sewing summer clothes,
You ride on the cow's back blowing your flute,
Spring has climbed up the tree crowning the hill,

Do not forget meeting me in the backyard last night."

He witnesses their faces burned deep red,   25
He witnesses their backs bent in winter time;
Not long ago they, too, had their own children,
Replaying the role of their ancestors.

He has become sick of watching one old thing after another,
The old pine on the hill, the new bridge on the river;   30
He hopes some day will be special--
The special day finally comes.
[First published in *Golden House Monthly* No. 7, 1929]

二百年的老樹

在那廟前,水邊,有棵老樹,
光光的腦袋,縐縐的皮膚,
他張開了手臂遠望青山,
像要說訴他心中的悶苦。

二百年前在這裏種了根,
便從未曾動過一寸一分,
他看著一所所村屋切牆,
他看著一所所村屋變粉;

他看著幾十百對的男女,
最初都睡在母親的懷裏,
吮著乳,哭,笑,小眼睛張閉,
不久便離了母親去田裏。

待到男的長大,女的長美,
他們便會在樹蔭下相會,
一個忘記了田裏的鋤犁,
一個忘記了鍋裏的飯菜。

"我騎在黃牛背上吹小笛,
你坐在竹籬邊上制夏衣,
春天快跨上那山頭樹頂,
別忘了今晚上到後園去。"

"我坐在竹籬邊上制夏衣,
你騎在黃牛背上吹小笛,
春天已跨上了山頭樹頂,

PART TWO: TWENTY-FIVE POEMS

別忘了昨晚上在後園裏。"

他看著他們的臉兒透紅,
他看著他們彎了腰過冬;
沒多時他們也有了兒女,
重複地扮演他們的祖宗。

他已看厭了,一件件舊套,
山上的老柏,河上的新橋;
他希望有一天不同平常,
有不同平常的一天來到。
(首刊於1929年《金屋月刊》第7期)

25. The Newly-Wedded Bride

The Question

Alas, the newly-wedded bride crowned with jewels,
All glory belongs to you tonight;
Yet what makes you feel so sad?

Tonight's love serves as the sun,
Vaguely devoted in your breast;   5
Yet what makes you feel so sad?

Your receptive yet shut close-shut lips,
Would be better with a man's kiss;
Yet what makes you feel so sad?

You should ride upon Jupiter's joyful arrow,   10
Wet with your virgin's blood,
Yet what makes you feel so sad?

The Reply

Ah, you ask me why I feel so sad,
It is my sorrow for myself;
How can I stop feeling sad for a moment?   15

Brightness has left my dark breast,
From this garment of evil draped over it;
How can I stop feeling sad for a moment?

PART TWO: TWENTY-FIVE POEMS

The seeds of calamity were planted very early by another,
Just now six pairs of eyes have been wedded;   20
How can I stop feeling sad for a moment?

How pitiful this deluded bridegroom!
He will sleep with an adulteress unaware.
How can I stop feeling sad for a moment?
[First published in *Sphinx* (Shihou) No. 2, 1928]

新嫁娘

問

啊珠寶冠下的新嫁娘，
一切的榮耀今夜屬你；
你還有什麼事要悲傷？

今夜的愛情當如太陽，
暖暖地貢獻給你胸膛；
你還有什麼事要悲傷？

你迎情而緊閉的唇上，
當添一個男性的吻香；
你還有什麼事要悲傷？

求必得的快樂的箭上，
當將你處女的血沾染，
你還有什麼事要悲傷？

答

咳你要問我為甚悲傷，
這原是我獨有的痛創；
我怎能有一忽不悲傷！

光明離我黑暗的胸膛，
從此披了罪惡的衣裳；
我怎能有一忽不悲傷！

PART TWO: TWENTY-FIVE POEMS

禍殃兒早有別人種上，
方才是六隻眼睛拜堂；
我怎能有一忽不悲傷！

只可憐這糊塗的新郎，
他將與一個淫婦同床；
我怎能有一忽不悲傷！
（首刊於1928年《獅吼》半月刊第2期）

Appendix A: Shao Xunmei's Translated Poems
附錄 A：邵洵美的英譯詩

1. Worry by To Fu

The Country is torn to pieces, but rivers and hills
And cities are like the wilderness in Spring.
The flowers shed tears for my sorrow;
While birds remind me of hateful partings.

For three months the fight has been fighting on,　　　5
A letter would now be dearer than thousands of gold pieces:
Alas, I have been worried! My hair is white,
And much too short for flowers or hair pins.
[Published in *Candid Comment* No. 1, 1938]

春望 (杜甫)

國破山河在，
城春草木深。
感時花濺淚，
恨別鳥驚心。
烽火連三月，
家書抵萬金。
白頭搔更短，
渾欲不勝簪。

2. The Butterfly's Love by Li Ching-Tsau

The night was long, though happiness was short:
Dreaming of Chang-an, I tried
To recognize all its songs and streets;
Should Spring come with good news,
And the moon and the flowers lead me to him.   5
Dinner is lovely, though the dishes are simple:
Wine is a beauty, and the plums are intoxicating.
Let everything happen as I wish!
Let the flowers not laugh, when I drunkenly kiss them.
Pity us, who will soon be as old as Spring.
[Published in *Candid Comment* No. 1, 1938]

蝶戀花 (李清照)

永夜懨懨歡意少，空夢長安，認取長安道。為報今年春色好，花光月影宜相照。
隨意杯盤雖草草，酒美梅酸，恰稱人懷抱。醉莫插花花莫笑，可憐春似人將老。

3. A Poem by Su Tung-P'o

I am an old man, and yet I wear a flower in my hair!
I am not ashamed, because I have a thick-skinned face!
But I see the flower is blushing on my head.
To find itself in such an unfitting place!
I am drunk, and need someone to lean upon as I walk home;
It will give the pedestrians a pleasant surprise.
At least half of the window-curtains will be lifted up,
And pretty girls will peep at me with admiring eyes!
[Published in *Candid Comment* No. 1, 1938]

吉祥寺賞牡丹 (蘇東坡)

人老簪花不知羞，
花應羞上老人頭。
醉歸扶路人應笑，
十裏珠簾半上鉤。

4. Magnolia Flower by Yan Shu

When the swallows and wild ducks fly over
The Spring too passes,
As I think of my drifting life, thoughts crowd my heart.
By how many hours is this life
Longer than the Spring season?   5
How are they scattered? Like autumn clouds: how soon they
    disappear.
Oh, I have heard the violins: I've loosed the girdles of the sa-
    cred girls,
I pulled at their sleeves, even tearing them, but I could not
    hold those maidens….
Let us not be the only ones who awake,   10
It is better to lie drunk among the flowers
And leave the rest to Fate.
[Published in *Candid Comment* No. 1, 1938]

木蘭花 （晏殊）

燕鴻過後鶯歸去，細算浮生千萬緒。
長於春夢幾多時？散似秋雲無覓處。
聞琴解佩神仙侶，挽斷羅衣留不住。
勸君莫作獨醒人，爛醉花間應有數。

Appendix B:
A Chinese Swinburne: Shao Xunmei's Life and Art[1]
附錄 B：中國的史文朋：邵洵美的人生與藝術

Jicheng Sun and Harold Swindall

No one today except for a handful of scholars of modern Chinese literature has ever heard of Shao Xunmei (1906-1968), who is deserving of attention both as a man and a poet, translator, publisher, editor and essayist. Only a few Chinese scholars have written anything about him, and Chinese reference books merely give him a few lines as a minor poet with decadent tendencies; clearly, he is officially not to be regarded as signifying anything special in the country's literary history. Outside of China, Shao has also received scant attention: googling his name reveals several articles chronicling his affair with the American writer Emily Hahn, but there are only a couple of scholarly articles about him online, and there is no Wikipedia entry for him. A search on Amazon leads to two studies with chapters devoted to Shao, and perhaps half a dozen others that mention him in passing. This neglect is wrong, since Shao Xunmei was the epitome of a movement in 1930s Shanghai that aimed to reinvigorate the rest of China with a new culture derived from the energies of the European decadence. In his case, the inspiration came especially from Algernon Charles

---

[1] For more, please find the book *The West in Asia and Asia in the West: Essays on Transnational Interactions*, Editied by Elisabetta Marino and Tanfer Emin Tunc, McFarland & Company, Inc., Publishers, Jefferson, North Carolina, 2015, pp.133-145.

Swinburne, under whose influence he lived and wrote. Ultimately he failed as first the Japanese and then the communists had greater force, but Shao still stands as a representative of a certain moment when many Chinese artists looked westward for models, and he achieved a unique East-West synthesis in both his life and his art.

Works Cited

Chen, Zishan, ed. *Selected Works of Shao Xunmei (Xunmei wencun)*. Liaoning Educational Press, 2006.

Du, Xianzhi. "Five Issues on the Study of Shao Xunmei." *The Journal of Huzhou Normal College*. 1988(4): 43-46

Fruehauf, Heinrich. "Urban Exoticism in Modern and Contemporary Chinese Literature." In *From May Fourth to June Fourth: Fiction and Film in Twentieth-Century China*. Eds. Ellen Widmer and David Der-wei Wang. Harvard Contemporary China Series, 1993. 133-64

Hutt, Johnathan. "The Sumptuous World of Shao Xunmei." *East Asian History*, No. 21 (June 2001): 111-142.

Lee, Leo Ou-fan. *Shanghai Modern: The Flowering of a New Urban Culture in China, 1930-1945*. Harvard University Press, 1999.

Li, Guangde. "The Poems and Criticism of Shao Xunmei." *The Journal of Huzhou Normal College*, 1985(2): 1-9

Shao, Xiaohong. *My Father Sinmay Zao (Wo de baba Shao Xunmei)*. Shanghai Bookstore Publishing House, 2005

Shao, Xunmei. *Works of Shao Xunmei (Shao Xunmei zuopin xilie)*. Shanghai Bookstore Publishing House, 2008. Vol. *Hua yiban de zui'e*

"Theophile Gautier." Dictionary of Art Historians. Web. 8 July 2012. www.dictionaryofarthistorians.org/gautiert.htm

Xiandai Xuesheng, first issue. In Zhu Ziqing, ed. *Zhongguo xin wenxue daxi: shiji*. Shanghai Liangyou Tushu Chubanshe, 1936.

Zhang, Yinde. "*Les Sociabilites litteraires Shanghaiennes des annees 1930: le cas de Shao Xunmei*." In Nicolas Idier, ed. *Shanghai:*

WORKS CITED

Histoire, promenades, anthologie et dictionnaire. Paris: Robert Laffont, 2010. 617-35

HOMA TITLES ON CHINA

9780966542103	Flower Terror: Suffocating Stories of China
9780966542127	The Peony Pavilion: A Novel
9780966542141	Butterfly Lovers: A Tale of the Chinese Romeo and Juliet
9781931907033	Ink Paintings by Gao Xingjian, Nobel Prize Winner
9781931907026	Splendor of Tibet: The Potala Palace, Jewel of the Himalayas
9780966542172	The Dream of the Red Chamber: An Allegory of Love
9781931907156	Breaking Grounds: The Journal of a Top Chinese Woman Manager in Retail
9781931907163	The Eleventh Son: A Novel of Martial Arts and Tangled Love
9781931907231	Paintings by Xu Jin: Tradition and Innovation in Chinese Fine Brushwork
9781931907255	China's Generation Y: (HC)
9781931907323	China's Generation Y: (PB)
9781931907248	Willow Leaf, Maple Leaf: A Novel of Immigration Blues
9781931907422	The Holy Spark: Rogel and the Goddess of Liberty
9781931907439	Journey across the Four Seas: A Chinese Woman's Search for Home
9781931907446	The Bitter Sea
9781931907460	September's Fable
9781931907507	From Ironing Board to Corporate Board
9781931907514	The Chopsticks-Fork Principle x2: A Bilingual Reader
9781931907521	Everything I Understand about America I Learned in Chinese Proverbs
9781931907538	The Art of Mogao Grottoes in Dunhuang
9781931907682	China's Terracotta Army and the First Emperor's Mausoleum
9781931907545	Two Lifetimes
9781931907552	Seven Kinds of Mushrooms
9781931907620	Folk Culture in China's Zhejiang Province
9781931907569	Educational System in China
9781931907576	Educational Policies and Legislation in China
9781931907583	Basic Education in China
9781931907590	Higher Education in China
9781931907606	Technical and Vocational Education in China

HOMA TITLES ON CHINA

ISBN	Title
9781931907637	The Legend of Haibao 1: The Myth of the Crystal Palace
9781931907644	The Legend of Haibao 2: A Journey of the Gourmet
9781931907651	The Legend of Haibao 3: Meeting Friends from Afar
9781931907668	The Legend of Haibao 4: A Journey through Space
9781931907774	A Concise Illustrated History of Chinese Printing (HC)
9781931907675	A Concise Illustrated History of Chinese Printing (PB)
9781931907743	Managing China's Modernization: Perspectives on Diplomacy, Politics, Education and Ethnicity
9781931907781	The Three Character Classic (2nd Edition): A Bilingual Reader of China's ABCs
9781931907798	Beauty of Stone Windows: A Cultural Interpretation of Stone Windows of Sanmen
9781931907804	Teaching Chinese the American Way
9781931907811	Disappearing Shanghai: Photographs and Poems of an Intimate Way of Life
9781931907828	Understanding China's Criminal Procedure
9781931907835	Chinese Civil Procedure and the Conflict of Laws
9781931907842	Reading the Times: Poems of Yan Zhi
9781931907897	The Illustrated Book of Chinese Tea
9781931907903	Salt in Ancient China
9781931907910	Decoding Critical Genes of Enterprises: The Bionic Laws for Organizational Longevity
9781931907941	The China Well-being (Minsheng) Development Report 2012
9781931907316	The Historical Architectural Map of Beijing
9781931907200	Jack Ma: Founder and CEO of the Alibaba Group
9781931907750	Chinese Art since 1980: Oil Painting 1
9781931907958	Chinese Art since 1980: Oil Painting 2
9781931907965	Chinese Art since 1980: Traditional Chinese Painting 1
9781931907972	Chinese Art since 1980: Traditional Chinese Painting 2
9781931907989	Chinese Art since 1980: Engraving • Watercolor
9781931907996	Chinese Art since 1980: Sculpture • Pottery Art • Mural
9781622460137	Watercolor: Paintings by Zhejiang Artists
9781622460144	Farmers' Art: Paintings by Zhejiang Farmer Artists
9781622460151	Pan Honghai: A Chinese Oil Painter
9781622460168	Sun Yong: A Traditional Chinese Painter

HOMA TITLES ON CHINA

9781931907866	Shaolin Kungfu
9781931907873	Taijiquan
9781931907880	Chinese New Year Painting
9781622460014	Anshun Local Drama in China
9781622460021	Dehua Porcelain in China
9781622460038	Huzhou Writing Brush in China
9781622460045	Mount Tai Steles in China
9781622460052	Silk and Bamboo Music in Southern China
9781622460069	Bronze Drums in China
9781622460076	Folk Legends of Gengcun in China
9781622460083	Quanzhou String Puppetry in China
9781622460090	Cantonese Opera in China
9781622460106	The Glove Puppet Show in China
9781622460113	Sichuan Opera in China
9781622460120	Violet Sand Crafts in China
9781622460175	Confucius Says: A Novel
9781622460199	The Quasi-War in East Asia: China's Dispute with Japan over the Ryukyu (Liu-Ch'iu) Islands and Its Global Implications
9781622460205	The Science of Human Settlements in China
9781622460212	The Stories of Tea
9781622460229	Yiwu, China: A Study of the World's Largest Small Commodity Market
9781622460236	The Verse of Shao Xunmei
9781622460243	The Art of Chinese Couplets
9781622460250	Chinese Folk Tales: Volume 1
9781622460267	Chinese Folk Tales: Volume 2
9781622460281	The New Travels of Marco Polo: Hans in Zhejiang

www.homabooks.com

www.ingramcontent.com/pod-product-compliance
Lightning Source LLC
Chambersburg PA
CBHW032022230426
43671CB00005B/171